MR. HOLLAND STRIKES BACK
MORE MUSICAL TALES FROM THE PODIUM

TREY REELY

FOREWORD BY FRANCIS McBETH

Copyright (C) 2002 by Trey Reely.
All rights reserved.
Published 2003. Paragould, Arkansas.
Printed in the United States of America

Requests for permission to make copies of any part
of this book should be mailed to:
Trey Reely • 1200 Spring Grove Road • Paragould, Arkansas 72450

No part of this book may be reproduced in any form including amateur and professional recordings, motion pictures, recitation, lecturing, public reading, Websites, radio and television broadcasting, translation into foreign languages, meditation, use at birthday parties and bar mitzvahs without expressed written permission of the author.
For more information on how to purchase additional copies visit
http://www.sculptnet.com/reely/

Grateful acknowledgment is made to
The Instrumentalist Company, Northfield, Illinois, for permission to reprint Trey Reely's articles: "Call of the Wild" [previously titled "Payback Time"] (April, 2001); "Every Band Has One" [previously titled "This Cast of Characters Appears in Every Band"] (January, 2000); "Beginning Band Solo Titles and the Self-Esteem of Beginning Band Students" [previously titled "Bye, Bye Barbie"] (April, 2000); "Reality Check" [previously titled "Talking with Teenagers"] (September, 1999); "My Hero" (June, 2000); "Double (Reed) Trouble" [previously titled "Marching Oboes?"] (August 2000); "The Politically Correct Band Director" [previously titled "The Language of Band"] (March 1995); "Murphy the Band Director" [previously titled "Murphy's Law Applies to Music"] (September, 1994); "Dear Santa" (December, 1999); "Lots of Wind from PDQ Bach" (March, 2000); "It Goes Without Saying" [previously titled "Speechless at Last"] (August 2001); "Student Conductors" [previously titled "Giving Students Conducting Lessons"] (January 1995); "Convention Fatigue" [previously titled "Of Clinics, Ballads, and Boredom"] (December,1998).
(Subscribe to *The Instrumentalist* for 1 year, 12 issues for $24 (US Delivery)
200 Northfield Rd, Northfield, IL 60093 847-446-8550)

Author photo (see back cover) by Wayne Garner of Garner Studio.
Cover design, editing, and prepress by
SculptNet Web Site Development, Inc. — www.sculptnet.com
Audra Howerton, President & Creative Director
Roger Oliver, Illustrator

No animals were hurt in the production of this book.
Any resemblance to people living or dead is
probably more than just a coincidence.

ISBN 0-9673756-1-4

Library of Congress Catalog Card Number: 2002093301
Music-Humor-Education-Essays-Conducting-Band

Other Books by Trey Reely

Move Over Mr. Holland: Insights, Humor, and Philosophy on Music and Life

What people are saying about *Move Over Mr. Holland*

"It made me both laugh and cry."
 — *Jamie Bishop*
 University Student

"I read it all in one day."
 — *Claude Smith*
 Band Director — Searcy, Arkansas

"It started out as bathroom reading material, but was so good I moved it to bedside reading material."
 — *Tracy Meadows*
 Band Director — Piggott, Arkansas

"A great source for the teacher. Students, spouses, relatives, and friends will love it as well. When you pick it up, be ready to start a book you won't put down."
 — *Eldon Janzen*
 Author, The Band Director's Survival Guide

"This book should be on every music teacher's desk as a quick pepper upper."
 — *Earl A. Schreiber*
 Reviewer, International Trombone Association

"Mr. Reely's book, *Move Over Mr. Holland*, is a must-read for any music teacher or for that matter any musician. The well-written stories are timeless and

strike all the right chords and wrong notes that any music teacher lives with on a daily basis. Often under his more humorous messages is a hard kernel of truth."
— *Joe Bonner*
Assistant Professor of Music — Arkansas State University

What people are saying about *Mr. Holland Strikes Back*

"*Mr. Holland Strikes Back* is a must-have book for the library of every band director. The series of vignettes in the book range from the humorous to the philosophical to the how-to. Trey Reely is able to create humor from the serious and insight through the humor. His tongue-in-cheek insights allow us to laugh at ourselves, our students and their parents, our colleagues, and just about everyone who ever even thought about a high school band. I particularly found a great deal of wisdom through jest in '25 Ways To Mess With A Band Director's Mind' and '25 Ways Directors Can Get Back at Students!' We have all been there! Get the book now!"
— ***Kenneth R. Raessler, Ph.D.***
Director and Professor, Emeritus—School of Music, Texas Christian University

"I could not help but constantly nod my head in agreement while reading *Mr. Holland Strikes Back*. Trey Reely takes a 'nobody could make this up' look at our profession. This book serves as a great stress reliever and has some very pointed ideas that can be helpful to the young band director."
— ***Dr. William Clark***
Professor of Music—New Mexico State University

"Whether for inspiration or sheer entertainment, Trey Reely's *Mr. Holland Strikes Back* perfectly describes the joy and humor of the band director's myriad roles."
— ***John Knight***
Oberlin Conservatory of Music

"Here is a must-read for all music educators. Trey Reely's sequel to his popular *Move Over Mr. Holland* is just plain brilliant. With *Mr. Holland Strikes Back*, Reely brings you into his fraternity and then whimsically brings you out of self pity. Sandwiched between humorous incidents is a philosophy worthy of Plato and wisdom worthy of Solomon. It makes me wish I had been a music educator instead of a band historian!"
 — *Dr. Paul E. Bierley*
 Author, John Philip Sousa: American Phenomenon

"College students and new band directors would greatly benefit from Trey Reely's practical advice."
 — *Ann Sewell*
 Associate Professor of Music, Emeritus — Harding University

"*Mr. Holland Strikes Back* provides valuable information for school band directors. Readers can expect to find many helpful suggestions clothed in good humor. Directors should buy this for their administrators!"
 — *Dr. George E. Baggett*
 Professor of Music Education, Emeritus — Harding University

"This collection of real-life events reminds us that band directors are cast in a role of much more than just teachers of tone, rhythm, and pitch. Those who weather the years in the music profession find themselves fulfilling the role of mother, father, and counselor without quite realizing that the college senior methods course hardly touched on the subject of human relations. Not unlike the movie that

introduced us to Mr. Holland, this book brings the set to life, and in this case you can be assured that the script is true."
— *Eldon Janzen*
Author, *The Band Director's Survival Guide*

"Trey Reely has taken the frustrations, difficulties, achievements, and joys of being in band and turned them into an engrossing, funny, and captivating book. With intimate, detailed, and witty observations, he has set the bar higher for the rest of us in this genre."
— *Tom Batiuk*
Creator, *Funky Winkerbean*

"Trey Reely struck a humorous chord with his popular book *Move Over Mr. Holland*, and he goes one step further with *Mr. Holland Strikes Back*. Anyone who has had anything to do with the band community will appreciate Trey's amusing perspective of the band world. Sometimes we have to laugh to keep from crying."
— *Tim Lautzenheiser*
Motivational Speaker

Contents

Dedication	xv
Acknowledgements	xxi
Preface	xxv
Foreword	xxix
Call of the Wild	1
Every Band Has One	6
Beginning Band Solo Titles and the Self-Esteem Beginning Band Students	14
Name That Instrument	20
Reality Check	27
My Hero	34
Double (Reed) Trouble	38

The Politically Correct Band Director	43
Murphy the Band Director	48
My Favorite Things	78
Monday Night Football	80
Dear Santa	91
The Fine Art of Publicity	96
Ready or Not—Your Final Test	102
Lots of Wind from PDQ Bach	120
Granddaddy's Baton	127
Fables in 4/4 Time	134
The Mind of the Wiseguy	140
My Fifteen Minutes of Fame in Reader's Digest	147
Classic Poetry Revisited	151
Bladder Trouble	161

To the Rear	164
Real World University	168
The Band Director Game	174
It Goes Without Saying	176
Selections from My Private Journal	180
Coda: Practical Suggestions for Directors	185
Open Letter to Piano Teachers	186
Student Conductors	188
Convention Fatigue	193
Theory X or Theory Y	199
Likes and Suggestions	207
Beginning Band Night	211
Creative Beginning Band Classes	218
Appendix A: On The Selection of Music for the Marching Band	224

Appendix B Basic Discipline Tips	230
Appendix C The Handshake	233
Typeface	245
Epilogue	246
Index	249

Dedication

Just the mere thought of an unpleasant task produces the profoundest fatigue in me. I refer to this malady as Assignment Induced Fatigue Syndrome (AIFS). When I was a student, this manifested itself in long periods of procrastination on homework assignments, particularly on major reports and projects. One of my most severe cases of AIFS occurred in seventh grade when it took me weeks to summon up enough energy to put together an insect collection. Despite my affliction, I did manage to tell my mom about the assignment the day before it was due, and she was understandably perturbed. She would have none of this "AIFS business," as she called it. To her it was just plain LAZY. Despite her consternation, she agreed to help me. I assured her that an insect collection couldn't be too hard to complete in one

evening. Our mission seemed fairly simple: locate, kill, impale, mount, and identify fifty insects.

Finding the insects was not a big problem. At nightfall, Mom and I stood on the front porch snatching as many bugs as we could from around our lone porch light. Mom seemed to grow more annoyed with each bug that she captured, repeatedly muttering, "If you ever wait until the last minute again, so help me I'll . . ." She never would finish the sentence, but I knew it wasn't something I would want to hear anyway.

After gathering our fifty bugs, we poured alcohol on them to ensure their preservation. We couldn't tell if the alcohol was doing any good—it seemed only to make them hopelessly soggy. At this point our difficulties had only just begun. Impaling a soggy insect is a lot harder than it appears. Bugs that managed to survive their capture and alcohol dousing somewhat intact crumbled in our hands. Wings, legs, heads, antennas, thoraxes, abdomens, eyeballs, and stingers . . . name a body part—it came off. We had enough parts to create three new bugs.

Once we had positioned the impaled bugs on the board, Mom and I were faced with our final task— identifying the insects. Armed with a *World Book Encyclopedia*, we religiously attempted to find each insect's illustration or description. This conscientious effort soon gave way to finding any insect that looked even remotely like one of our victims and recording that as the identification. We then adjusted the names to fit the various missing parts: the headless mosquito, the one-winged moth, the legless firefly, and the severed porch beetle, to name a few. When that failed, we would make things up—concocting terms like paterno bugiopolis, orientalis kamikaze moth, and Alabama dung wasp.

With the identification completed, Mom and I were able to sit back and observe our work. For a last-minute project it really looked like, well, a last-minute project.

The next morning as I lugged my project to school, I couldn't wait to see my friends' projects. Many of my friends were also stricken with AIFS and were sure to have some sorry-looking projects like mine. It was going to be fun comparing stories of how difficult it was to do the project in one night.

To my chagrin, my friends presented models of perfection! How could they do this to me? Where did they learn this? Were their parents entomologists or something? Did they order projects from *National Geographic*? Traitors.

As I looked at their projects, I saw insects striking magnificent poses rivaling the finest statues of the Renaissance. It was almost as if the bugs purposefully gave several choices before freezing in a final dramatic pose. And not only were they magnificently posed, they were perfect specimens, captured right after some type of body-building event for small invertebrates. The bugs in my neighborhood just didn't eat right, I conjectured. That would explain the crumbling body parts.

My mom was unbelievably patient with me as I battled AIFS on and off for over twenty-one years. She helped me complete endless projects: a paper mache' Saturn, a leaf collection, an oil well constructed from toothpicks (don't ever try this), Cub Scout pinewood derby cars (while my Dad was in Vietnam), and church sermons. Without her great typing skills, I would never have finished school term papers. In college, I had a problem narrowing my term paper topics down to manageable lengths; I wrote a report on all forty of Mozart's operas. Mom is lucky Mozart died when he did, or she might still be typing!

I am not even sure if I thanked Mom at the time. Maybe I assumed all mothers were so helpful. After having taught for many years, I now know better. And while our projects were not always the neatest, most high-tech, professional quality projects to go down in

Dedication

the annals of science, I know that they were made with love. Thanks, Mom.

By the way, I received an "A" on my project. I'm not sure why — either it was because my teacher was tenured and senile or she hated to see the bugs suffer in vain. Also, my AIFS is in remission now, except that it flares up some when the grass in the front yard gets tall.

Acknowledgements

There may well be only two categories of people who read acknowledgements: people who know the author and suspect he may mention their name or anyone who has ever written a book. I never read the acknowledgements page until after I wrote my first book, and I now read it faithfully because I know I am reading about special people—individuals who collectively make what can seem like an impossible task not only possible, but successful.

First, my wife Ronda for her continued patience, support, and encouragement. My kids Ashton, Ryan, and Kelsey who all three helped type the original manuscript.

Talented friends who helped edit were Ellen Meadows, Suzette Killough, Karen Church, and Kyle Liddell. I want to particularly thank two former professors of mine, Ann Sewell and Dr. George Baggett, for their help in the preparation of the manuscript (I even added a few humorous lines at Dr. Baggett's behest). My colleagues at Paragould High School,

Carla Wilcox, Bonnie Hamilton, Doris Hagen, and Lori Dial for their grammar and punctuation tips.

Those who were willing to read the manuscript despite their busy schedules and offer a kind word or two: Ken Raessler, John Knight, Bill Clark, Eldon Janzen, Paul Bierley, Tim Lautzenheiser, and Tom Batiuk.

Francis McBeth, a most gracious man, for his willingness to read the manuscripts of my first two books and write a foreword for this one, despite a very hectic personal schedule. I am honored to have his thoughts in this book.

Kudos to my colleague and friend Terry Hogard for his help in proofing the final manuscript.

I take the blame for any errors still left in the book. My editors were great, but I think I gave them so many mistakes to find, it quite possibly could have worn them out!

Pat Averwater of AMRO Music Stores in Memphis. Pat was nice enough to be an early promoter of my last book.

Cathy Lenzini, former senior editor of *The Instrumentalist*, whom I enjoyed working with for several years before she resigned to spend more time with her newborn.

Acknowledgements

My in-laws, Ron and Maxine Huddleston, for raising such a wonderful daughter, providing such a beautiful spot on the lake for me to write when we visit, and serving as an unofficial distributor for south central Texas.

All band students, past and present, who serve as the source for many of my stories.

Illustrator, Roger Oliver.

Finally, Audra Howerton, band parent, friend, and Creative Director at SculptNET.com, for her helpful professionalism. Without her great work, my first two books probably would never have materialized.

Preface

I have been fortunate to have a number of articles published in music journals. As a result, colleagues have expressed an interest in getting published and have asked my advice. I usually suggest they start with a letter to the editor. Here are some ways to get published and possibly stir up a little controversy while you're at it!

The Anti-Marching Band Letter
Send this letter to a magazine in June, so it can be published just in time for another marching season. This will draw very strong sentiments and evoke letters from those who like marching band. Be sure to stir the fire a little by writing things like "marching band has no educational value whatsoever," and "competition has no place in music and directors who delve deeply into marching competitions are simply greedy and despicable trophy hunters."

The Disgruntled Reader Letter

After listing your lengthy qualifications (real or imagined), mention as many inaccuracies in a particular article as you can. Expound upon any philosophical differences you may have with an author's opinion. Write arrogantly and forcefully and don't forget to cancel your subscription at the end of the letter. [1]

The Eagle-Eye Letter

Write a letter criticizing a particular photo used that displays a poor embouchure or hand position. Better yet, criticize the cover photo.

The "I Live in Siberia and Need Music" Letter

One sure way to get published is to develop sympathy. After giving your pitiful budget figures, mention that the only music your band has on file is your collection of incomplete transcriptions of Haydn baryton solos.

---

[1] I had the privilege of having a disgruntled reader letter aimed at me. The letter was more humorous than the article I wrote, though that certainly was not his intention. The writer didn't catch any of the subtle or overt humor. See the chapter "Double (Reed) Trouble" for the source of his contention.

Call of the Wild

I know why band parents rarely say, "Thank you." It's because of the scars they still bear from when their kid was in beginning band. They find it hard to thank someone who not only forced them to shell out several hundred dollars for a glorified noisemaker, but also doomed them to years of nighttime mayhem. Most parents were happy with the quiet solitude of their evenings as they read or watched television to relax after the labors of the day. All this became but a memory when that shiny instrument arrived. They can't help but wonder how such a beautiful instrument can wreak such aural havoc. They probably have doubts that their little darling will ever sound any better (some do and some don't).

The variety of tone colors that beginning woodwind players are able to create is simply amazing: the hollow wail of the flute, the psychotic shriek of the clarinet, the exploding air released from the embouchure of an oboe player who cannot produce a sound on a new reed, the impersonation of a leaking balloon by the bassoon, and the klaxon-like honk of a saxophone. I believe the clarinet was the inspiration for the knife-thrusting motif of Bernard Hermann's *Psycho* theme, probably because one of his children played clarinet in beginning band.

> My domestic refuge, my sanctuary of solitude, my haven of rest became a musical maelstrom.

Few woodwinds can match the versatility and nausea-inducing capabilities of the brasses. Arguably the most sickening sound is that of the brass player with a neck, throat, and jaw so tight that it brings to mind the last bit of toothpaste being squeezed from the tube. (And we wonder why substitute teachers never return.)

Beginning low brass players lucky enough to have a more open sound most closely resemble the moose at different stages of maturity. The euphonium (meaning beautiful sound, ha!) is the fledgling calf finding its voice. The trombone is an adolescent moose

The "Do You Know Where I Can Find . . . ?" Letter

Looking for an obscure piece of music? Write a letter like the following: "I am looking for an arrangement of some music that I heard as background music on a radio show commercial in the 1930's and was later used on merry-go-rounds at many participating McDonald's restaurants. Does anyone know where I can find this?"

The Effusive Praise Letter

Find something you like in a previous issue of the magazine and eloquently extol its virtues: "I have been teaching for forty years and that is the best article I have ever read on developing finger muscles in oboe players. The article changed my life."

The Confusion Reigns Letter

Write and ask the editor to clarify some particular point in an article that you found confusing: "In your January article, 'Fundraising for Fun and Profit,' the author stated that orange and grapefruit sales can reap great profits. Were these California or Florida citrus? Which are better?"

The Memory Lane Letter
Write how much the article reminds you of some great moment in your life. If the article spoke of a particular individual, mention how you met the individual once in an airport terminal bathroom and how it remains the highlight of your life.

Hopefully, these suggestions will get your creative juices flowing. If you need a little more help, may I suggest you start by sending a letter to *The Instrumentalist* saying how much you enjoyed this book. Just a suggestion.

Foreword

Trey Reely's first book *Move Over Mr. Holland* was a wonderful account of the trials and joys that all directors of bands have encountered. *Mr. Holland Strikes Back* leans a bit more toward the serious side of our profession but still has many moments of wit and humor.

I say a bit to the serious side because of the chapter entitled, "My Hero," where he talks about the life of a former student, James Harrison, who died in a commercial airline crash. James was also a student of mine at Ouachita Baptist University where I taught him freshman theory. James survived the crash but was killed after going back several times into the plane to save others. James was the kind of student that makes our chosen work so gratifying.

The chapter, "Granddaddy's Baton," is particularly poignant as Trey describes how his banddirecting grandfather's baton helped heal wounds in their relationship. I still have my mother's baton, and I would be interested in learning which one is longer.

Having had to choose titles for fifty years, I was particularly interested in Trey's insight on the effects of titles on students in the chapter entitled "Beginning Band Solo Titles and the Self-Esteem of Beginning Band." There is a fine line between a good title and a bad one, and this chapter makes many good points. I think the saddest title I ever heard was a song Mac Davis wrote in the 50's. It was called "Drinking Christmas Dinner."

In the chapter, "Every Band Has One," you will be able to put a name from your own experience on each entry. I enjoyed the chapter, "Real World University," because we all have wondered why we face so many situations that we never heard of in college. Of all the conductors I studied with, not one taught me a most important technique that I needed when I conducted a professional orchestra—how to come off stage and hug rich widows without getting sweat on them.

This book is filled with so much useful information given with good humor that I enjoyed every word. I heartily recommend this book for its humor, advice, and renewed memories.

—Francis McBeth, Composer

that shouts for joy when it discovers it can add vibrato to its plaintive calls. The tuba completes the circle of moosely life with its more mature but dying attempts at producing a low B♭.

The upper brasses complete the menagerie. Schizophrenic trumpet players who cannot hit a second line G in class become a herd of bellowing elephants when dismissed. The little monsters yodel sounds rivaling Johnny Weismuller in early Tarzan films. Even at such an early stage, young French horn players display their uniqueness. Not content to sound like an ordinary cow, the player brings forth sounds so exotic, so noble, so like the last breath of an antelope in the throes of death.

Finally, there are the giants of auditory assaults, the percussionists. In theory they use the practice pad at home, but these soon become casualties in bandroom Frisbee games and they substitute more resonant objects.

And if the individual sounds aren't terrifying enough, mix all of them into the musical brew, and the songs in the typical beginning band book take on new dimensions. London Bridge falls down with a reading of 9.2 on the Richter scale, Aunt Rhodie's old gray goose dies after one last valiant honk, the hot cross buns melt in the fire, and Mary's little lamb goes with her to band one day and never returns.

Over the years I have learned to tolerate these musical assaults, confident in my ability to change that weak, nasal, and unfocused tone into a strong, blaring, and unfocused tone. But I was ill-prepared for an assault of sound within my own home. Yes, it was payback time for me. Thousands of band parents were exacting their revenge.

Our daughter, who selected flute, was the first to join band. Other than some harmonic exercises and high notes, things were not too bad, except for the dog, that is. We thought he was singing along, but our vet tells us that from the look of his eardrums he was probably howling in agony.

The next year the assault increased when our seventh-grade son started on euphonium and our fifth grade son, not to be outdone, decided to learn the trumpet early. My domestic refuge, my sanctuary of solitude, my haven of rest became a musical maelstrom. From the tolling of the first period bell to the click of the last lamp retiring for the night, I had no peace.

Once I wondered why parents didn't say thank you. Now I consider myself lucky that at least a few don't hate me. I'm not even sure if I like myself. Although the future may not hold another thank you, I have a new response for the few I might receive. Instead of replying, "You're welcome," I will say, "No— thank you!"

Every Band Has One

Every band is certainly unique in character, but there are features of its individual members that most certainly exist in all groups in one form or another. My only hope is that we never have them all at once! Here's a look at a few.

Cool Claude. A comedian, clown, and practical joker, Cool Claude is loved by fellow students, and the director likes him even though he wants to ring Claude's neck. He is usually a trumpet or trombone player who stands a good chance of becoming a band director in a few years.

Quinn the Quitter. Quinn doesn't wait until the end of the school year to quit. He decides to quit the day of an important band performance.

Missy the Mouse. Missy is very shy and reclusive. A third clarinet player, Missy's worst embarrassment is having her name called out at marching practice. Even one such incident causes lifelong trauma.

Tardy Teddy. Teddy is late to every rehearsal and performance. He has an alarm clock that "malfunctions" every other day. When other students pick him up, he makes them late, also. Talking to his parents is a waste of time because they always run late, too. Poor Teddy must be a victim of genetics.

Billy the Brown-Noser. The band director loves him because he does all of the dirty work no one else will do, but no one else likes him. Billy wants to be a band director when he grows up.

Gary the Grim Reaper. Poor Gary has a relative die right before every concert (sometimes five grandmothers in one year).

Louie the Loader. A low brass player, Louie takes pride in moving and loading all the heavy equipment. He always does this with a smug look on his face which suggests that trumpet players are wimps.

Danny Dogpile. Danny is a third trumpet player who is solely protected by the band director's liability concerns; otherwise, the director could give the word and fifty band members would knock him over and pile on. Danny draws such vehemence by his incessant need to make stupid remarks that no one finds funny (except him, of course).

Priscilla the Prima Donna. Priscilla's hair is perfectly coiffed. In fact, everything about Priscilla is perfect.

Getting her hair sweaty during marching practice almost sends her to a mental hospital. She is a first chair flute player who also owns her own piccolo.

Vinnie the Virtuoso. A trumpet player, Vinnie doesn't care if the trumpet section is any good as long as he gets his solos. Vinnie dates Priscilla the Prima Donna. They plan on marrying after their solo careers and having children with perfect pitch.

Hanna the Hypochondriac. Hanna can injure herself opening a package of Pop Tarts. She consistently misses performances due to an unlimited variety of ailments.

Annie the Air Head. Annie likes to ask questions, usually dumb ones. Oddly enough, and to everyone's surprise, Annie is an extremely talented first chair flutist.

Ernie the Expert. Ernie has moved in from another school. Ernie constantly tells everyone how the band in his last hometown was so much better than this one and how his other band was ranked number one in the continental U.S. Ernie is usually a terrible musician whose other band got even better when he left.

Bad Luck Lou. Poor Lou. His instrument breaks before every chair test. Any mistake he makes is due to a sticking valve, stuck pad, or unsoldered joint.

Forgetful Frank. Frank is always forgetting something. He loses enough music to start a new library. Someone is always "stealing" his music. Sometimes his instrument is even stolen, only to reappear two days later.

Lovestruck Laura. Laura is more concerned with having a boyfriend than any musical endeavor. If she doesn't have a boy to sit by on the band trip, her life's almost not worth living.

Punctual Polly. Polly is a rarity—she shows up for everything thirty minutes early.

Evelyn the Excuse-Maker. Evelyn has never made a mistake in her life, but she is the victim of an amazing string of unfortunate circumstances.

Distracted David. With his mind on more important things, David has never heard a band announcement in his life. He asks you questions about matters discussed just five minutes before.

Van the Vulture. Van is a nice guy—it's just that he wants your job. Extremely goal-oriented, he plans to major in music education.

Godfather Gil. You can count on a visit from Gil's parents whenever he is unhappy. They claim you just don't like the poor kid and remark that "boys will be boys" when questioned about Gil's boorish behavior.

Chip on the Shoulder Chip. During marching rehearsal, asking Chip to move over a half-step causes a major outburst. He wonders why you didn't ask all the other people out-of-line to move over, too.

Solo Wannabe Willie. Willie bugs you every year to give him a solo during marching band until you finally relent his senior year, and he muffs it.

Greg the Griper. Greg gripes about everything. What's interesting is that he does nothing to help solve the problems he points out.

Libby the Leader. Libby takes initiative and makes things happen. She leads by example, working harder than anyone in the band.

John Doe the Dependable. John Doe is always there. Quiet in nature, he never gets in trouble and never misses a rehearsal. Although he is not an outstanding performer, John always works hard to learn his music. Directors wish they had a whole band of students like John.

Bladder Bill. A freshman, poor Bill has the world's smallest bladder. Thirty minutes must be added to every trip to account for extra bathroom stops just for Bill.

Lucy the Leveler. Lucy is a sharp kid with a quick wit. She keeps the director humble with barbed, yet good-natured, comments on everything from his style of dress to impending baldness.

Party Hardy Harold. A third trumpet player, Harold is in band to socialize. Harold sometimes misses a rehearsal but never a band party.

Sarah Sunshine. Sarah is that happy-go-lucky student who brightens your day just by coming into the band office to say hello.

Sally Spirit. Sally loses her voice at every football game. She doesn't understand anything about football but spreads her infectious enthusiasm by screaming anyway. At heart she is cheering for the band.

Beginning Band Solo Titles and the Self-Esteem of Beginning Band Students

Don't be fooled by the sophisticated title of this chapter (sounds like a dissertation title, doesn't it?). It is written in jest. Of course, if you would like to write a dissertation on this topic, be my guest.

Every spring, bands across the land are participating in solo and ensemble competitions. During this time, band directors have a greater opportunity to shape the personalities of their students than they ever could have suspected. Have you ever wondered why the players of each instrument exhibit identifiable personality traits? In some ways it may be a "chicken or the egg" issue, but if you take a look at the various solos our students have the opportunity to play, you can see that their titles could easily affect a kid's psyche.

Take flute solos for instance. It's hard enough to get a boy to play the flute in the first place, and then what happens when solo and ensemble season comes around? They get to play solos with titles like "Little Waltz," "Le Petite Danse," "Reflections," and "Echo Song"—not exactly manly fare. And what do they have to look forward to when they get older? Flute ensembles that all have the word "dance" in them— "Dance of the Reeds," "Dance of the Sugar Plum Fairies," and such. By the end of the first year, my male flute players want to switch to something else. What boys need are titles like "Women Magnet March," "March of the Macho Man," and "Biceps on Parade."

Clarinetists face similar problems. Boys may not even know what titles like "Le Petite Rien" and "Valse Felice" mean, but they know it's nothing macho. And you can forget any title with the word romance in it— you might as well just call the piece "Barbie Doll Walk." While boys don't avoid the clarinet like the flute, think how many could be attracted to it if pieces were titled "Hunks on the Loose," "Slam Dunk Blues," or "Monday Nitro."

Is it any wonder that boys flock to the trumpet and then develop an ego the size of New York? It's because they get to play solos that display a noble heritage and character: "Fanfare," "Helios," "Valiant," "Apollo," and "Venture." They even get to chill a little with "When the Saints Go Marchin' In." Saddle them with solos like the flutes and clarinets have and you'd see their heads shrink in a New York minute.

Pity the poor oboe players. What do they get to play? Songs that all imply something creepy, foreign, and snake-like. "The Glow Worm" and "Song of India" are standard fare for aspiring oboe players.

There is even a piece called "The Organ Grinder." How would you like to play a song that would be most suitable for accompanying a poor little monkey as it begs for pocket change? The snake concept wouldn't be so bad if a piece were called "A Snake for Jake," "Deadly Cobras," or something similar.

Bassoon players have it even worse. If they are lucky enough to find a piece to play at all, the title makes it hardly worth the effort. How will the bassoon ever shed its second class, buffoonish image with titles like "The Clown" and "The Sorcerer's Apprentice"? Titles like "Down with Clowns" and "Blood-Curtaling Screams" (a curtal is an early ancestor of the bassoon) would help give bassoonists more toughness and confidence.

Of all the woodwinds, the saxophone players have some reason to think they are the most hip members of the band. This is because they get to play jazz-oriented tunes like "When the Saints Go Marchin' In," "Jazzin'," and "Cool Blues." There are also some rather interesting titles like "Fox You Stole the Goose" and "The Cuckoo" that, unfortunately, sometimes prove rather prophetic.

While trumpet players often exhibit an exuberant boastfulness, horn players display a more subtle yet no less arrogant sense of self. Why? Because of the long, noble pedigree indicated by the solos they get to perform: "The Huntsman," "Greensleeves," "Summer Song," and "The Hunt." Maybe horn players would loosen up a little if they got to play such songs as "Those Wild and Crazy Horns" and "Horns Unplugged."

There is no doubt as to why trombone players are an unbridled and off-the-wall bunch. With pieces called "Camping Out," "Hot Taco," and "Trombone Tapioca," this is natural. If they had selections called "Little Waltz" or "Waltz Miniature," even they would be ready to sign up for the disciplined world of ballet.

Why do tuba players generally grow into large behemoths with forearms the size of a trumpet player's thighs? Look at what they get to play their first couple of years: "The Jolly (i.e., fat) Farmer Goes to Town," "The Jolly Coppersmith," "Jolly Jumbo," and "The Elephant Dance." And when the titles don't have them bouncing around like a happy, overstuffed pig, they are sleeping the day away with "The Lazy Lullaby" and "Slumber Song." Just reading those titles makes me want to go out and eat a triple Whopper, up-sized fries, and a milkshake before sleeping for three days.

> Is it any wonder that boys flock to the trumpet and then develop an ego the size of New York?

And I suppose the most downtrodden band members of all are the baritones (pardon me,

Beginning Band Solo Titles and the Self-Esteem of Beginning Band Students

euphoniums), particularly the treble clef euphoniums who already feel like they can't read music since it's not bass clef. To make matters worse, the bass clef baritone often gets trombone music, and the treble clef baritone gets trumpet music like some kind of musical hand-me-down. Solos with titles like "Keep Your Greasy Hands off MY Solo" and "I Am Eupho Hear Me Roar" could rebuild their badly damaged egos.

While titles of wind music tend to be less creative, percussion titles have long been on the edge. In fact, they actually need to be toned down a little. Titles like "To Buzz or Not To Buzz," "Flim-Flam-Fun," "Torch Drive," "Flameout," and "Ruffing up a Storm" tend to whip young drummers (pardon me, percussionists) into an adolescent frenzy. With more titles like "Lose This Music Blues," "Responsibility," "Silence is Golden," and "Soft Sounds on Parade," they would soon become civilized.

Until publishers and composers realize the cause and effect relationship between solo titles and young musicians, it is solely up to directors to sift out the dangerous pieces each spring and avoid the psychological abuse to our students. If I seem a little over-concerned, it is probably because of the ongoing trauma from my first trumpet solo, which was titled "Paranoia."

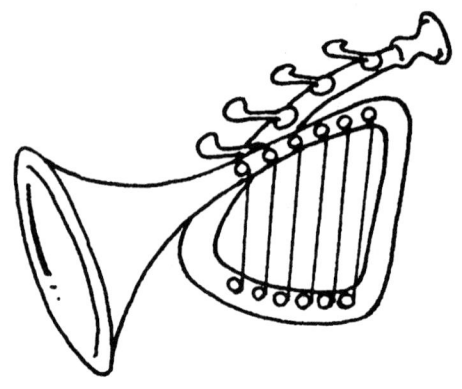

Name That Instrument

You know a musician truly loves his instrument if he names it. Eric Clapton had his Brownie and BB King his Lucille. I feel bad because I never gave my instrument a name. Maybe I would have been a better player if I had named my trumpet. Giving it a name may have enabled us to bond more. Sadly, my trumpet was stolen several years ago and is now nothing more than a lost instrument with a serial number. If I had named it, I could have put something like "answers to the name of Timmy" in lost and found ads.

Although I regret the intimacy I lost by not naming my instrument, there *was* one advantage. I have noticed that such personalization makes a relatively mundane instrument repair more like major surgery on a close relative. I had a student once who dropped his tenor saxophone and mourned deeply as "Herbie" spent two torturous weeks in the repair shop. He asked me every day if Herbie was better yet. After several weeks of this verbal Chinese water torture, I screamed, "It's a saxophone, not a human being!" I was being rather insensitive but felt much better nonetheless.

I have not, however, encountered a student who has named an instrument *after* himself. Instrument inventors, on the other hand, have named instruments after themselves for hundreds of years. The Albisifono invented by Abelardo Albisi (I'm glad he didn't call it the Lardophone), the Bussophone by Busson of Paris, the Antoniophone by Antoine Courtois, the Bigophone by the Frenchman Bigot, the Gabusifono by Gabusi of Bologna and the Mullerphone by Louis Muller are a few examples.

Probably the most prolific at this practice was Adolphe Sax, one dude who was definitely full of himself. He couldn't wait to put his name on anything he touched. Saxophone, saxhorn, saxtromba, saxtuba — you name it, he named it (after himself). Adolphe was not fully to blame, however, since he was merely following a practice begun by Sax Sr. who created namesakes like the cor saxomnitonique and the trombono saxomnitonique. I'm just glad his name wasn't something like Charles-Joseph Belch.

While naming an instrument after oneself does seem slightly vainglorious, the practice generally results in, at worst, a rather boring, yet suitable name (see below for some exceptions). Many other instruments, however, were doomed to failure just by their names. It is obvious that modern marketing techniques were not at work. Here are a few examples:

Bimbonifono (Giovacchino Bimboni)— Try getting a girl to play that instrument!

Burumamaramn (see also vurumbumbum)— Can you imagine being a conductor and sounding like you're trying to start a motorcycle every time you ask them to play?

Trompeta bastarda— Don't trumpet players get called enough names without something like this?

Nose flute— I can just see the ole boys sitting around a campfire till one drawls, "Any of you boys wanna hear a little 'Home on the Range' on my nose flute?"

Spitzfloete — We all know there is an element of spit in playing an instrument, but why make it obvious?

Globular flute — Sounds like something made of gelatin.

Ferryphone (Armand Ferry) — Try getting a boy to play this!

Heckelphone (W. Heckel) — Probably popular at early twentieth-century athletic events and comedy clubs.

Hellhorn (Ferdinand Hell) — One would have to be above a certain age just to tell people that he played this.

Herhorn — Early victory for feminists as there was no himhorn.

Sackbut— Fortunately it's known today as the trombone. I have a hard time getting kids to play the trombone as it is. Could you imagine the giggles during a recruiting session at an elementary school today if a director had to say, "Who would like to play the sackbut?" I'm sure it sounds rather romantic in French, but something gets lost in translation.

Dung— Trumpet players will be quite humbled to know that this is a Tibetan trumpet. You won't catch me putting my lips up to anything with a name like that.

Tambor terrero— This is a Spanish ground drum. I find it interesting that the word terror was associated with percussion instruments in Spain long before school bands existed in America.

Dumb Piano— This is a name our kids call our keyboard on days they don't want to practice. I didn't realize there was some historical precedence for that.

One characteristic of inventors that I have gathered from my scattered reading on the subject is their obsession with invention—a churning mind that never stops. Inventors came up with new instruments while making others instruments, resulting in names coming straight from the toolbox.

Musical Saw— I can't wait to see the development of the modern equivalent—the electric musical chain saw.

Nail Violin— Many stressed-out parents would probably like to create a modern version by nailing their kid's violin to the wall just out of reach.

Hammerklavier— Beethoven preferred this German name over the term pianoforte. Pianoforte sounds a little more musical to me, but who am I to argue with the master?

Anvil— Wagner uses eighteen of these in his opera *Das Rheingold*. (No kidding.)

Inventors took the idea of playing with their food to new heights. This created some rather interesting monikers.

Sausage bassoon— Did a performer play this at breakfast time while a colleague played an egg bassoon?

Onion flute— Did this one make people cry when they played it (or maybe when they chopped it up)?

Quart bassoon— Obviously much easier to handle than the gallon bassoon (or the European liter bassoon).

Crumhorn— Sounds like something made from leftovers.

I admire the creativity of early inventors. Today there are probably many undiscovered instruments right under our nose flutes, but we just don't see them. It's time for lunch; I think I'll see what instrument ideas I can get from a slice of bologna—parts from ten different instruments combined into one, perhaps?

Reality Check

Concentrate. This has to be one of the most common directives band directors use each day. Each summer I formulate new ideas on how to improve my band's concentration and performance. It is a real challenge to get young people to maintain their focus to the extent that they will take the necessary steps to reach an important goal. In some ways, it is like trying to get a dozen five-year-olds to walk in a straight line.

Why is it so difficult? To get a clue, just put your feet up sometime and have a conversation with one of your students. When was the last time you had a *real* conversation with a teenager? I had a real eye opener a few years ago. I was talking to an All-State baritone player in my band and, as sometimes happens, she brought up the subject of boys. She talked about rather typical boy-girl problems (not being much of a Dear Abby or Dr. Drew I would just grunt every now and then to let her know I was listening), but I did a double take when she mentioned that during our pre-halftime warm-up the week before (where we stand in a circle and tune), she couldn't remember the notes to our opener because this boy she liked kept looking at her. *This was an All-State player.* What in the world were the other players thinking? I had fooled myself into thinking that my students were actually listening to my Vince Lombardiesque speeches!

Another thing that makes it hard to get through to kids is that they just don't take things seriously enough. Combine this with the fact that directors can take things *too* seriously, and conflicts are inevitable. I find it hard to be too terribly critical after I reflect on my high school days where lapses of concentration and seriousness were all too common. I remember marching practices where my high school band director would be approaching a nervous breakdown, hastily repairing all the fractured formations he could at the last minute. While he would frantically scurry around, students marching behind him would abandon their traditional high-knee march and begin a rocking Florida A&M style we thought was cool. As soon as he turned their way, they would revert to form, and the other side would undergo its stylistic transformation. Back and forth it would go until we considered it too risky to continue. (He never did catch on, as I recall.)

Sometimes more serious circumstances make concentration difficult. At an away game one year, we had just arrived, and as I was getting the band ready, I noticed the smell of alcohol. I quickly ruled out the junior high director, student teacher, and drum major. That left a father who had just arrived with his daughter, one of my sophomore clarinet players. He told me that he was taking his daughter home directly after the game because he didn't think the city we were playing in was safe. He then proceeded to stand in front of the band for the first and second quarters,

> Band can help students develop a mental toughness in a society that has increasingly made us softer and less willing to roll up our sleeves and get our elbows dirty.

constantly looking up in the stands at his daughter. (Apparently there was a boy in the clarinet section whom he didn't want her to talk to.) As halftime approached, I asked the daughter if her dad had been drinking, and she confirmed that he had.

After halftime I talked with the father, urging him to let his daughter ride the bus for safety reasons. When he did not comply, my assistant contacted our principal and the police. After an extended ordeal, the police agreed to let another band parent drive the father home while his daughter rode the bus. My fears were relieved somewhat, but I wondered what would happen to her when she got home. She assured us that she could go home without any fear of danger and after talking to her sister and mother on the telephone, I agreed.

I found out that the father had a history of drinking which explained why the daughter had come up to me a couple of times that year and said she might not be able to attend a ballgame because her dad wouldn't let her go and might make her quit. She was too embarrassed to say he was an alcoholic. It was a real struggle for her to get to some of our ballgames, much less concentrate when she arrived.

The ideas we impart on a daily basis must coexist with the silly, innocuous, and sometimes very serious elements of our students' lives. It is within this context that band can be of great benefit. Requiring great concentration despite other pressures will better prepare them for the future. A common characteristic of great athletes, actors, and performers is the ability to focus deeply on the task at hand, shutting out all negative thoughts. Computer companies readily hire musicians because of their ability to concentrate and pay attention to detail. Band (particularly marching band) can help students develop a mental toughness in a society that has increasingly made us softer and less willing to roll up our sleeves and get our elbows dirty. In an increasingly "feel good" society, students learn the value of doing things whether they really feel like it or not.

During a recent hot summer practice, one of my freshmen sousaphone players half-jokingly observed that "holding this sousaphone all day builds character." Unlike this freshman, many students don't readily recognize these benefits until many years later, but we can speed the process along by identifying these benefits during the course of their high school careers. Comments about their improving focus, mental toughness, and other positive characteristics allow them to see more purpose in what they are doing and can also serve as a source of great pride.

It is also important, however, to recognize band within the context of a teenager's life. I once heard a clinician say, "I don't care who plays the solo, because the music is all that matters." I (and my students who were there) felt rather demeaned by the statement. The music is *not* all that matters, and your students will certainly figure out whether that is all that matters to you, either by word or deed. While we fight battles against notes, rhythm, articulations, and a host of other musical challenges, our students struggle with many problems we can only imagine. Students should see that we care about musical excellence *and* them.

Spend some time each year getting to know your students better. Informal settings are the best time. Whether it's a band party, sitting around after a band practice, or eating lunch with them during summer practice breaks, find out things about your students that have nothing to do with music. Ask them questions about their likes, dislikes, pets, family, and hobbies—and above all show how much you care by listening attentively.

In *Tyranny of the Urgent,* Charles Hummel tells us that we shouldn't let the urgent take the place of the important in our lives. As we begin each school year, the urgent tasks are everywhere; make sure they don't replace what is truly important and lasting. This is not too difficult—if we just concentrate.

My Hero

On a stormy June 1, 1999, a commercial jet crashed and caught fire while attempting to land in Little Rock, Arkansas. This was another tragic headline to most people, but it hit close to home with me. Some of the passengers on the flight were members of a choral group from Ouachita Baptist University in Arkadelphia, Arkansas, who were returning from a trip to Europe. Among the nine dead was a former saxophone player in my band, James Harrison.

James began studying music as a seventh grader in the fall of 1989, the first in his family to do so. His father remembers wondering what his child was getting into by signing up for band. James's dedication to music was clear from the start, and he developed into a fine saxophonist and a dedicated band member. His attitude and wry sense of humor made him a pleasure to work with. At graduation in 1995, he was awarded the Donald R. Minx Director's Commendation Award, an honor each year for the student who exhibits the ideals and musicianship that most contributed to the success of the band. James enrolled at Ouachita Baptist as a music ministry major.

I know from experience that two of the most difficult aspects of losing a loved one are the fear of forgetting details of the person and a sense of guilt when the pain fades. Music cannot answer all the whys of life, but it can help us to remember and heal.

> The way James lived his life each day prepared him for the decision he made in a time of crisis.

I am sure others close to James will think of him many times as they sing a hymn he loved. My memories will center around a particular piece, Frank Ticheli's *Cajun Folk Songs*. I have a recording of James performing the alto saxophone solo that opens the first movement. Ironically, the first movement, "La Belle et le Captaine," centers around the idea of death: a young girl feigns death to avoid the advances of a captain. All I need to do is listen to this piece, and I hear James speaking and telling me that because of his Christian faith, he too is only feigning death.

Music often urges us to resolve and remember, rather than to torture ourselves with unanswered questions.  Over time, the dissonances will turn into consonances as the good memories of James overwhelm the tragedy surrounding his death. Many composers have written works to eulogize the loss of loved ones. While some compositions eulogize the loss of individuals with long, productive lives, others mourn the loss of a young life— one cut off before its chance to fully blossom: Lo Presti's *Elegy for a Young American* is dedicated to the memory of John F. Kennedy, and Andrew Boysen's *I Am* is written in memory of a high school student who died tragically. Such works as these do not cause pain as much as they allow us to work out pain in a rehabilitation of the soul.

James may never have a composition written in his honor, but James wrote his own composition each day of his tragically-shortened life. His very life was a short masterpiece, an *Elsa's Procession to the Cathedral* or a *Salvation Is Created*. While many have longer lives, often with periods of waste and mindless wandering, much like an ill-conceived symphony, James's life was a work of musical economy. Each note carried maximum importance.

James spent his summers as a church youth and music minister serving others, which no doubt encouraged others to do likewise. Witnesses to the crash reported that James survived but remained on the plane to save others and lost his life in the process. In March of 2000, James was posthumously awarded the Kiwanis International Foundation Robert Connelly Medal for heroism.

The act of heroism surprised no one who knew him. I have never believed that heroes just happen. The way James lived his life each day prepared him for the decision he made in a time of crisis. Just as a well-written composition uses each note and phrase to build to a musical climax, so too did James's life build to the decision that he would remain and help others. His example gives me the hope that in the beginning band each fall I may find another hero in the making.

Double (Reed) Trouble

I witnessed a depressing scene several years ago at the Arkansas Open Marching Championships. An oboe player from a participating high school won third place in the best soloist category. Imagine that, an *oboe* player won third place soloist in a *marching* contest.

I might not have been so disturbed if the oboe player had marched with the oboe during the entire show—that, I admit, would have been quite a feat. However, this player set his clarinet down, took an oboe in hand, played "Princess Leia's Theme" from *Star Wars* and went back to the clarinet again. It was like seeing a football team send in an 85 pound kicker with three seconds to play to decide a hard-fought game played by 300 pound behemoths.

Even worse, the solo had to be miked. Brass players would never tolerate being amplified. Miking a brass player would be like putting elevator shoes on Shaquille O'Neal or a weight belt on Roseanne Barr.

It is probably clear by now that I am a brass player, but I like oboes. I really do. It's just that they need to know their place—which is inside. Oboe players might argue that the oboe's antecedent, the shawm, was played in town bands for outdoor occasions, particularly in the 1300's, but I would dismiss their argument on the grounds that it is too downright scholarly. Besides, oboe players don't even like marching band. They would much rather spend their time carving up new reeds with their special little oboe tools, listening to Vivaldi concertos, and dreaming of landing a recording contract for an elevator company.

Allowing an oboe player to perform at a marching festival is a dangerous and revolutionary precedent. I am sure that seeing the oboe soloist gave

> **My trombone soloist, Bubba, went into shock when he was outscored by this oboe player.**

some bright ideas to other oboe players attending the contest. My oboe player, who once suffered stage fright performing in front of her deaf grandmother, bellyached about how she never got a solo in marching band. Don't oboe players have enough pressure mounting in their brains without entertaining such delusions of grandeur?

If this revolution spreads uncontrollably, what will be the ultimate cost to the egos of brass players? Being outscored by an oboe player at a marching contest is like a woman being a runner-up to a man at the Miss America Pageant or a piano soloist being a runner-up to an accordion player in a concerto competition.

My trombone soloist, Bubba, went into shock when he was outscored by this oboe player. Although trombone players seem to be an insensitive lot, their psyches can be rather fragile at times. Bubba said that losing the solo competition was worse than the day his sister beat him in arm wrestling or the time his truck was drubbed in a drag race by a Volkswagen Beetle. Bubba also said he had a recurring nightmare in which he was being stalked across the football field by hundreds of oboe-bearing Princess Leias with giant cinnamon rolls on each side of their heads.

Double (Reed) Trouble

Today Bubba still has a tendency to go into a rage when he hears an oboe, but I assure him that most band directors can relate to that and he will just have to live with it. His therapist is making some progress.

All I am asking for here is a little compassion and fairness. When was the last time you saw a trombone player cut in on a woodwind quintet? Or a tuba infringe on an oboe duet? Or a trumpet player break in on a woodwind trio? Trumpet players sometimes play oboe solos with mutes, but that's not their fault.

As you enter each marching season, please consider keeping oboe players in their little world of chamber music and leaving marching band to the big boys. You'll never see me putting my oboe player front and center of the marching band. Unless, of course, he can play like that kid at the Arkansas Open.

The Politically Correct Band Director

One cannot be too careful these days — misspeak once and you could be looking for another job. Here are some politically correct terms you can use to make sure you are never required to attend sensitivity training sessions.

articulatorally disadvantaged — 1. unable to play correct articulations 2. the inability to double or triple tongue

acoustically dispossessed — an ensemble playing with poor balance

artistic baton manipulator — majorette

coordinationally different — 1. majorette who consistently drops the baton 2. color guard member who is consistently out of sync

creatively deprived — unable to write interesting drill

deferred maintenance — failure of the school's maintenance department to perform required minor repairs

digitally challenged — unable to move the fingers fast enough on difficult musical passages

dysfunctional marcher — student who is consistently out of step

educational postal literature — junk mail

embouchure impaired — poor embouchure

freshpeople — ninth grade band members

intervallically disoriented — 1. in performing, playing the incorrect harmonic 2. in marching, consistently maintaining the wrong interval between marchers

intonationally inconvenienced — playing with poor intonation

knowledge-base nonprocessor — beginner

limited muscular capabilities — poor endurance

maternal artistic baton manipulator — majorette mother

memory impoverished — forgetful student

motivationally deficient — lazy

negative attention getting — misbehavior in class

non-traditionally ordered — maintaining a messy band locker or cubby hole

previously recounted humorous narrative — old joke

processed tree carcasses — music and music books

repair technician — repairman

rote-needy — poor sight-reader

rhythmically impaired — unable to play correct rhythms (also called "rhythmically different")

size-friendly — extra-large band t-shirts (also called "generously cut")

supplemental budget program — fund raiser

temporally challenged — chronically late

tonally deficient — playing with a poor tone quality

vehicle appearance specialists — band kids washing cars

vertically challenged — short; in music, the inability to play high notes *vertically deprived* — a student encountering problems with high notes

POLITICALLY CORRECT BAND WORKS

Come Sweet Death (Bach) — Come Sweet Terminal Inconvenience

Fanfare for the Common Man (Copland) — Fanfare for the Common Person

Hymn for Band (Stuart) — Her for Band

King Cotton (Sousa) — Royal Cotton (or Queen Cotton)

Miss Trombone (Fillmore) — Ms. Trombone

Procession of the Nobles (Rimsky-Korsakov) — Procession of the Nepotistic Oppressors of the Economically Disadvantaged

Solid Men to the Front (Sousa) — Solid People to the Front

Jesu, Joy of Man's Desiring (Bach) — Supreme Being, Joy of Personkind's Desiring

The Marriage of Figaro (Mozart) — Figaro and His Companion

Fantasy on a Negro Spiritual (traditional) — Fantasy on an African-American Spiritual

Old Comrades March (Teike) — Chronologically-Advanced Friends March

Night on Bald Mountain (Mussorgsky) — Night on Follicularly Challenged Mountain

Hebrew Folk Song Suite (Osmon) — Songs of Jewish Persons

Poor Wayfaring Stranger (Protestant traditional) — Economically Exploited Immigrant

Murphy the Band Director

Due to the Internet, this may be the most popular article I have ever written. I have found it on several websites and translated into two other languages. First published in *The Instrumentalist* in 1994, the article was not included in my last book because I had considered making it a separate book entirely. I decided not to do so and have included it here. Some of the laws have come from other sources, and I have kept their names intact to give them proper credit. Most of the others I have named for friends and colleagues. Forgive the indulgence of naming a couple after myself.

MURPHY'S LAW: If anything can go wrong, it will.

THE MURPHY PHILOSOPHY: Smile. Tomorrow will be worse.

O'TOOLE'S COMMENTARY ON MURPHY'S LAW: Murphy was an optimist.

THE EXTENDED MURPHY'S LAW: If a series of events goes wrong, it will do so in the worst possible sequence.

EVANS' AND BJORN'S LAW: No matter what goes wrong, there is always somebody who knew it would.

MURPHY'S EIGHTH LAW: If everything seems to be going well, you have overlooked something.

MURPHY GOES TO CONCERT FESTIVAL

LAW OF SELECTIVE ACOUSTICS: The percussion section will always come across as the loudest where the judges are sitting. It cannot be heard from the podium.

HATCH'S LAW OF CLARINET SQUEAKS: Clarinet squeaks will always occur in the most exposed sections of the music.

FILLMORE'S MARCH LAW: If a march can be rushed, it will.
> **COROLLARY:** A march rushes in proportion to a band's inability to play it quickly. That is, if a band cannot play it any faster accurately, it will rush.

BARTON'S INTERPRETATION PRINCIPLE: If you select one of four logical interpretations of a concert work, the three judges will like the other three better.

THE PLAY IT AGAIN SAM AXIOM: At concert festivals, at least three other bands will play your toughest selection.
> **COROLLARIES:**
> 1. All three perform before you do.
> 2. They will play it better.

SURPRISE SYMPHONY PRINCIPLE: At least one section of the music which the band has never had a problem with will go haywire.

CONTEST PRONUNCIATION PRINCIPLE: If a composition or composer's name can be mispronounced as the band's program is being introduced, it will be.

MURPHY PLAYS PERCUSSION

TROTTER'S LAW OF PERCUSSION MUSIC: Percussionists will consistently lose music, more as impending concerts approach.
> **COROLLARIES:**
> 1. All parts will be lost at least once.
> 2. They will not tell you it is lost until you catch them making up parts as they go along.

THE UNCERTAINTY PRINCIPLE: The location of all auxiliary percussion instruments cannot be known simultaneously.
> **COROLLARY:** If a lost percussion item is found, another will disappear.

PERCUSSION WILL NOT TRAVEL PRINCIPLE: One important piece of percussion equipment will be left behind in the bandroom on any given band trip.

PERCUSSION WILL TRAVEL PRINCIPLE: One important piece of percussion equipment will be left at the performance site.

DIMINISHING QUALITY EXCEPTION TO THE PERCUSSION WILL TRAVEL PRINCIPLE: If an important piece of percussion equipment is not forgotten, it will be switched with one belonging to another school.
    COROLLARY: The one you receive will be of lower quality.

LOST AND FOUND LAW OF DRUMSTICKS: Percussionist will lose sticks.
    COROLLARIES:
    1. Someone "stole" them.
    2. They will find them the day after you order new ones.

STIDMAN'S LAW OF DOOR CONSTRUCTION: The largest timpani is always four inches wider than the door to the auditorium.

MURPHY TRIES INSTRUMENT REPAIR

MURPHY'S INSTRUMENT LAW:
When an instrument breaks, it will be at the worst possible time.

> **COROLLARY:** The instrument will belong to a first chair player.

BALDWIN'S LAW OF INSTRUMENT DESTRUCTION: An instrument is easier to break than to fix.

WYSZKOWSKI'S LAW: Anything will work if you fiddle with it long enough.

LAW OF DIMINISHING REPAIRS: Restore one note on a woodwind and three others will go wrong.

MOUTHPIECE INERTIA PRINCIPLE: Brass mouthpieces are easier to render immovable than to dislodge.

HALBROOK'S LAW: A problematic instrument will work perfectly when a repair technician tries it.

LAW OF SELECTIVE OPERATION: Brass valves will stick on test days.
    COROLLARIES:
    1. They will not stick when the director tries them.
    2. They will stick when the student resumes playing.

THREE PRINCIPLES OF INSTRUMENT REPAIR:
    1. When needing to tighten a screw on a woodwind, the screwdriver with the correct size head will be missing.

    2. When needing to replace a woodwind pad, all available pads will be the wrong size.

    3. When a pad is accidentally dropped, it will roll to the least accessible part of the bandroom.

MURPHY ON THE MARCH

LEFT-RIGHT PRINCIPLE: At least one person is out of step in any one drill movement.

> **COROLLARY:** It is usually the same person.

MURPHY'S LAW OF MAJORETTES: If a majorette can drop a baton, she will.

> **COROLLARY:** She will be on the near sideline.

REELY'S FN-1 PRINCIPLE: Any piece you select as a closer will have a final note (FN) which is one step higher than your first chair trumpet player can play.

PETER'S PLACEBO: An ounce of image is worth a pound of performance.

THE WEATHER REPORT RULE: On game and contest days, bad weather reports are more often correct than good ones.

DARNED IF I DO, DARNED IF I DON'T PRINCIPLE: If the weather forecast is a downpour and you decide not to march at halftime it will miraculously clear. If you decide to march, it will begin to rain heavily on the drum major's downbeat.

SOUTHERN GLOBAL-WARMING PRINCIPLE: Temperatures the day before the first day of summer marching practice are in the low 70's and breezy. The first day of marching practice is 102 degrees with 100 percent humidity.

GLOBAL-COOLING PRINCIPLE: Temperatures the day before a Christmas parade will be in the 60's and dry. The day of the parade will be 5 degrees with sleet, hail, and snow.

SMALL BAND DRUM MAJOR DILEMMA: Your drum major will always be your best brass player.

THE PYTHAGOREAN EXCEPTION: $a^2 + b^2 = c^2$, except when trying to measure the corners of the band practice field.

NEW STADIUM MAXIM: Upon entering a stadium for the first time, bands which enter on the east side will invariably have seats on the west side.

RURAL VISITING BAND AXIOM: The stands for the visiting band will be decrepit and almost impossible to put the band on.
> **COROLLARY:** The stadium lights will be in front of the stands so that no one can see the music after it gets dark.

WIN-LOSS APPRECIATION EQUATION: The worse a football team's record, the more the fans like the band.

UNIFORM SHORTAGE POSTULATE: There will always be at least one band student who cannot find a uniform that fits.

FORGOTTEN UNIFORM PARTS LAW: At least one uniform part will be left behind on any given away game.

MEADOWS' LAW OF COMPUTER DRILL: You can still write lousy drill on a computer.
    COROLLARY: But it is much neater.

ELECTRONIC RATIO PRINCIPLE: The potential for disaster increases in direct proportion to how much electronic equipment is used in the halftime show.

HOLE IN THE SHOW LAW: After summer practices you will always be at least one person short of what you charted for the show.

CAMPBELL'S CLIMAX PRINCIPLE: When in doubt, do a company front.

REELY'S OBSERVATION ON DRILL DESIGN: The only thing worse than writing halftime drills is seeing what they look like after they are on the field.

MURPHY TRAVELS

BOGAN'S LAW OF BUS TRIPS: Bus breakdowns will always occur on the longest trips.

TRAVELING AMNESIA PRINCIPLE: Students will always forget something.

RT+1 PRINCIPLE: The scheduled return time (RT) of any trip will be one hour earlier than you actually return.
   COROLLARY:
   1. This happens even when you "pad" the return time with an extra hour.
   2. You will be late because of flute players with small bladders.

RT+3 PRINCIPLE: You will have to wait another two hours for the last parent to pick up his child.

TUNER WILL TRAVEL PRINCIPLE: On out-of-town performances, the tuner will be left behind.
   COROLLARY: If it is somehow remembered, the batteries will have run down.

MURPHY REHEARSES

MURPHY'S MUSIC STAND PRINCIPLE: The music stand you get will be the one that wobbles.

REELY'S ADAPTATION OF RAP'S LAW OF INANIMATE REPRODUCTION: If you take a music stand apart and put it together enough times, eventually you will have two of them.

CHALK ANOTHER ONE UP PRINCIPLE: There is always a piece of chalk and an eraser when you don't need them. When you need them, they have disappeared.

ANYTHING YOU CAN DO LAW: When something is done well, there are three trumpet players who think they could have done it better.

TWO PRINCIPLES OF DIMINISHING CONCENTRATION:
    1. Office aids will always interrupt rehearsal when concentration levels have finally reached their peak.
    2. Students late for class are always those who sit in the center of the band.

GIBSON'S LAW OF TEACHERS' MEETINGS: After-school teachers' meetings always occur the day of an important after-school rehearsal.

SHANAHAN'S LAW: The length of a teachers' meeting increases by the square of the number of teachers present.

WASHINGTON'S ASSEMBLY PRINCIPLE: Assemblies always occur during band rehearsal.

POST-CONCERT MAXIM: At least one instrument out of five will be left at home the day after a performance.

MISSING MUTE PRINCIPLE: At least one mute will be missing from the brass section at any given rehearsal.

WISDOM OF SOLOMON: If you can't say it, you can't play it.

EXTENDED REST THEOREM: The longer the rests, the less likely a section will enter after them.

DAVIS' DETERMINATION: Don't assume students will remember anything from one day to the next.

ASHTON'S LAW OF DIFFICULT MUSIC: Music which presents seemingly unconquerable difficulties will be disliked by students.

KIMBRELL'S SPECIAL REQUEST DILEMMA: When you wait until the last minute to hand out music especially requested by the superintendent, there will be no score, no first trumpet parts, and the piece is out of print.

MURPHY PERFORMS

McMURRAY'S PROGRAM PRINCIPLE: At least one name will be left off the concert program.
    COROLLARY: It will be the child of your building principal.

McMURRAY'S SECOND PROGRAM PRINCIPLE: If there are two ways to spell a name, the wrong one will be selected for the program.

GILBEE'S AWARD PRINCIPLE: When presenting awards, at least one student will be overlooked.

MURPHY'S LAW OF CLAPPING: If parents can clap at the wrong time, they will.
> **COROLLARY:** Half of the audience will giggle as the band continues playing.

INSTANT MUSIC CONCEPT: Administrators will ask the band to perform with very little notice, like you just have to wind-up the group and out the music comes.

TWO PRINCIPLES OF CYMBAL CUING:
> 1. Cue the cymbal player or he will not enter.
> 2. Cue the cymbal player and he still will not enter.

MURPHY THE FUNDRAISER

BOUNCING CHECK MAXIM: The check for the largest amount of fundraising items sold will bounce.

FUNDRAISING PRIZE PRINCIPLE: A third of all fundraising prizes received will not work and will have to be sent back.

FOWLER'S PROLONGED AGONY POSTULATE: At least one student will take six months to turn in fundraising money.
    COROLLARY: He will also try to turn in unsold items.

MURPHY SIGHT-READS

BLIND LEAD THE BLIND PRINCIPLE: Band students playing something correctly will almost always follow the students which are playing something incorrectly.

MURPHY'S LAW OF SMALL BAND SIGHT-READING: Invariably, the melody will, at some point, be in a voice which you do not have.
    COROLLARY:
    1. Cues will not be provided.
    2. If they are provided, they will be on the music of your weakest section.

WARNER'S SCORE MAXIM: You will have to conduct from a condensed score.

MURPHY COMPOSES

CHARLEY'S OBSERVATION: Computers were invented by Murphy.

TURNAUCKAS' OBSERVATION: To err is human, to really foul things up takes a computer.

SPEAR'S LAW OF PRINTING: Some errors will always go unnoticed until the music is in print.

O'CONNOR'S ADDITION TO SPEAR'S LAW: The first page the composer turns to upon receiving an advance copy will be the page containing the worst error.

MURPHY AT THE OFFICE

ROLLIN'S RULE OF ORGANIZATION: The more you plan, the more confusion when things go wrong.

TILLIS' ORGANIZATIONAL PRINCIPLE: If you file it, you'll know where it is but never need it. If you don't file it, you'll need it but never know where it is.

RICHARD'S COMPLIMENTARY RULE OF OWNERSHIP:

1. If you save something for future use, you will never need it.

2. If you throw an item away, you will need it as soon as it is no longer accessible.

EDWARD'S TIME / EFFORT LAW:

1. Given a large initial time to do something, the initial effort will be small.

2. As time goes to zero, effort goes to infinity.

COROLLARY: If it weren't for the last minute, nothing would ever get done.

COMMUNICATION PRINCIPLE: Letters sent home to parents will find their way to the following places:

15% left on music stands
25% left in music books or folders
15% left in instrument cases
15% left in lockers
15% under beds
15% parents receive

COPIER BREAKDOWN PRINCIPLE: Copiers will break down with only one more copy to make.

MURPHY'S BEGINNING BAND

NEW INSTRUMENT AVERSION LAW: If parents can find a cheaper, practically unplayable instrument from their Aunt Flotilla, they will.

TWO RECRUITING RATIO PRINCIPLES:
1. For every one student wanting to play clarinet, there will be six who want to play alto sax.
2. For every kid wanting to play alto sax, there will be seven who will want to play snare drum.

THE "THERE'S ANOTHER HOLE IN THE DAM" PRINCIPLE: Fix one spot in the music and another spot falls apart.

ALTERNATE AMNESIA AXIOM: Any alternate fingerings taught will be promptly forgotten.

TWO LAWS OF BEGINNING TROMBONE PLAYERS:
> 1. One out of every four trombone players you start will be hearing-impaired.
> 2. Beginning trombone players will use their spray bottles more on other band members than on their slides.

LOST AND FOUND PRINCIPLE OF BEGINNING BAND BOOKS: At least one beginning band book will be left on the music stand after class each day.
> **COROLLARIES:**
> 1. It will usually be the same student.
> 2. If it is not the same student, there will be no name in the book.

SWING IT AGAIN SAM LAW: If the dotted-eighth and sixteenth rhythm can be swung, it will.

SAY IT AGAIN SAM LAW: Even if everything is explained perfectly, there will still be a question.
    COROLLARY: You will have just answered the question one minute before it was asked.

BEGINNING BAND CONCERT LAW: There will be one video camera for every three beginning band members.

PREMATURE DEAFNESS RATIO: A director's hearing loss is directly proportional to how many percussionists are started each year.

GENERAL MURPHY

ELLEN'S MEDIA FAVORITISM LAW: There are always more pictures of the rival school's band in the newspaper than yours.

ARMSTRONG'S LAW: If you don't have it in you, you can't blow it out.

INNER GAME PRINCIPLE: Given enough instruction, any student can become totally confused.

THE TWO LEAST CREDIBLE SENTENCES IN BAND DIRECTING:
 1. The check is in the mail.
 2. One more time.

STERN'S OBSERVATION ON STUDENT MUSICIANS: Most hear what they think they are doing rather than what they are actually doing.

THE PUNCTUALITY PARADOX: Give a very strongly worded lecture about punctuality and you will be late to the next performance because of car trouble.

THE SOLO AND ENSEMBLE DILEMMA: Find the perfect solo for a student and the piano accompaniment is missing.
 COROLLARY: The piece is out of print.

THE CUSTODIAL PRINCIPLE: The band director's success with logistical concerns at school is directly proportional to his relationship with the custodial staff.

GREAT IS MORE LAW: Do a great job and you will be asked to do more.

BIDEWELL'S TRANSITION PRINCIPLE: You are never as good as the previous band director.

ANDERSON'S SHIFT THE BLAME SOLUTION: When in doubt, blame problems on the previous band director.

FESTIVAL HOST CERTAINTY: At least one entry form and check will be late for any given contest.
   COROLLARY: The check is in the mail.

TAYLOR'S PRINCIPLE OF INSTRUMENT PURCHASES: Buy a new instrument for the band one week and you will find a better deal the next week.

THE SALARY AXIOM: The pay raise is just large enough to increase your taxes and just small enough to have no effect on your take-home pay.

BAND BUDGET THEOREM: The budget one receives is inversely proportional to the size of the band program.

SCHOOL SCHEDULE LAW: If a new, more confusing school schedule can be developed, it will be.

COROLLARY: Band is opposite the only offerings of advanced courses.

POP MUSIC PRINCIPLE: A band student's practice time is directly proportional to how many copies of printed pop music he owns. More pop music means more practice.

TUBA WILL TRAVEL PRINCIPLE: Tuba players and other players of "exotic" instruments always move out of your district, not in.

NEW STUDENT LAW: New members of your band who have come from another city always play an instrument you have plenty of.

THE LOWEST COMMON DENOMINATOR PRINCIPLE: After a concert, parents will rave about how they loved the pop selection you played and will say nothing about the Grade 6 concert masterpiece.

PAPER-CUTTER PRINCIPLE: If you can splice off part of the marching music with the paper-cutter, you will.

MURPHY AND THE WIND FAMILY

WILD WEST TUNING PRINCIPLE: To get two flute players to play in tune, shoot one.

WALLER'S DEFINITION OF A NERD: Someone who owns his own E-flat clarinet.

ROSS'S DEFINITION OF A MINOR SECOND: Two oboes playing in unison.

DAUER'S TWO WAYS TO MAKE A TROMBONE SOUND LIKE A HORN:
    1. Stick hand in bell.
    2. Miss notes.

MEGHAN'S OBSERVATION ON THE DIFFERENCE BETWEEN A TRAMPOLINE AND A BASSOON: You take off your shoes before jumping on a trampoline.

TURNER'S OBSERVATION ON THE DIFFERENCE BETWEEN AN OBOE AND AN ONION: No one cries when you chop up an oboe.

HOGARD'S OBSERVATION ON THE SIMILARITY BETWEEN A SAXOPHONE AND A BASEBALL: People cheer when you hit either with a baseball bat.

KRZTON'S OBSERVATION ON THE DIFFERENCE BETWEEN AN OBOE AND A BASSOON: A bassoon burns longer.

My Favorite Things

One of my favorite things to read when I was a kid was *MAD* magazine because of the offbeat parodies. One that I remember in particular was a take-off on *The Sound of Music* titled *The Sound of Murder*. I've always wanted to write a musical, but Meredith Willson did it already with *The Music Man*, so I guess I will have to be content with my *MAD*-like parody of "My Favorite Things."

Cracked reeds and love notes all stuffed in worn cases,
Missed notes and rhythms, sly grins on kids' faces,
Fingers and horn valves all tangled in string,
These are a few of my favorite things.

My Favorite Things

Broken Manhassets and duct tape on tubas,
When my best flutist moves off to San Cruces,
Peddling band candy and pizzas in spring,
These are a few of my favorite things.

When the band plays, when the notes tune,
When the music flows,
I simply remember my favorite things,
And then my frustration grows.

Valve slides and mouthpieces all lodged in their places,
French horn harmonics, confused little faces,
Five hundred students who think I speak Greek,
These are a few of the things that just wreak.

Tantrums from parents, kids late for rehearsal,
Buses that break down or can't pass a turtle,
Budgets depleted so early in spring,
An old boss in new clothes who thinks he is king.

When the band plays, when the chords mesh,
When kids march like pros,
I simply remember my favorite things,
And then my frustration grows.

Monday Night Football

Al: We'd like to welcome everybody to our special halftime extravaganza. The Pittsville Plundering Pachyderms are with us tonight, and they are something really special. I turn now to my colleague, Dan Deerstand, and Dan, what do you think about these Marching Pachyderms?

Dan: Well, I tell you, Al. This is a great organization from top to bottom. Their director of bands, Bill "Jumbo" McCloud, does a great job, but he'll be the first to tell you that it could not be done without those valuable assistants. Their woodwind, brass, percussion, majorette, flag, rifle, drill team, and drum major instructors do a magnificent job. Not to mention the work done by the show designer, music arranger, junior high auxiliary helpers, equipment managers, and the bus and equipment truck drivers. And let's not forget about those amazing Pachyderm parents. With me now is my colleague Frank Gipper to tell us all about those amazing Pachyderm supporters.

Frank: Thanks, Dan. Yes, when you mention those Pachyderm band boosters you're talking about some special people. Just to get the band to the game tonight they sold 2,500 calendars, 1,000 light bulbs, and at last count, 4,313 toilet seat covers. And not only are these boosters real salesmen, they're like having a thousand cheerleaders in the stands. There's a whole sea of Pittsville Purple in the end zone wearing purple elephant hats and waving those trunks in eager anticipation of tonight's performance. Let's go down to the sideline to our own Brent Humburger to catch some of the excitement.

Brent: Thanks, Frank. I have the drum major, Joe Fermata, with me now. Joe, what's the band going to have to do tonight to win this halftime show?

Joe: We're gonna have to concentrate and execute in all phases of the show.

Brent: Good luck tonight, young man.

Joe: Thanks. Hi, mom!

Brent: Back to you, Al.

Al: Thanks, Brent. We are expecting a great performance tonight, but there have been some distractions this week which just might hurt tonight's performance. Here to discuss this with me is our special analyst, Nerve Cross. Nerve, you've watched them all week— what's the controversy about?

Nerve: There have been several problems plaguing the Marching Pachyderms. The first is the drum major controversy that flared up again last week when Joe Fermata, the current drum major, missed a piccolo cue and didn't land cleanly after his double flip off the podium on the show's finale. Chants of "We want Buck-y" could be heard from various parts of the home crowd. Bucky was Fermata's main rival at drum major tryouts last spring.

Al: So I guess Fermata has a lot on the line tonight.

Nerve: He does. But with a strong performance tonight he'll be back in the saddle again. I've heard from reliable sources that Fermata will do a triple flip into a split at the show's conclusion. If he doesn't land cleanly, Bucky will probably get the call.

Al: I heard the real problems this week have centered on the majorettes.

Nerve: Yes, Al. The majorettes have been upset all year, but it came to a head this week as they voiced their displeasure over their position on the football field. They claim their poor position on the field is due to the fact that their director doesn't appreciate them. When I questioned Jumbo McCloud about this, he said that he puts them on the goal line for the whole show so that end zone audiences could enjoy the show more.

Al: Has a compromise been worked out?

Nerve: Jumbo agreed to let them be featured on one number.

Al: Thanks, Nerve. I want to turn back to my colleague Dan Deerstand, and Dan, what kind of show are we going to see tonight?

Dan: From what I've heard, we're in for a real treat. The band will be opening with a Spanish number called "El Pachydermo." Their second number is a percussion feature, "Baby Elephant Walk," which will be followed by their production number, "Themes from *Dumbo*." And I am sure they will thrill us with their closer, "The Elephant," from Camille Saint-Saens' *The Carnival of the Animals*.

Al: Sounds like an exciting program. Well, the band is on the field and here comes the drum major to do his salute.

Dan: That was an outstanding salute.

Frank: I heard that he has been strongly influenced by Bruce Lee karate films.

Al: I see a trumpet soloist stepping out. It looks like he'll be starting the action tonight. What a nice sound!

Frank: That's Bill "Tenuto" Baldwin. They call him Tenuto because he holds his high notes a little longer than the rest of the band for effect.

Dan: Tenuto was highly recruited out of elementary school. His sixth grade recorder teacher said he was the best player she ever taught.

Al: He sure has the Pachyderms off to a fine start. The rest of the band has joined Tenuto in playing, and they've begun what looks like a very interesting drill.

Frank: The band is displaying some very fine posture out there.

Dan: This band has a reputation for being strong in the fundamentals. Look at them flex those feet as they do the glide step.

Al: Let's go down now to the field where Brent has a special guest with him.

Brent: Thanks, Al. I thought I would show you the specially designed marching shoe the Pachyderm band wears. I have one of the Pachyderm band mothers with me now who wears a pair for good luck. This is Marge Militaire. Marge, do you find these shoes comfortable?

Marge: Yes, very. The extra support in the heels makes them ideal for lots of walking. Hi, mom!

Brent: Back to you, Al.

Al: Thanks, Brent. The Pachyderms have started their percussion feature and it's Mancini's classic, "Baby Elephant Walk."

Frank: This is one of my favorite tunes—kind of reminds me of Dan!

Dan: Let's not start with the fat jokes, Frank.

Al: Break it up, you two. You're missing some great action on the field. There's some real precision marching going on out there.

Dan: The crowd's really getting into those flexing arcs.

Frank: The follow-the-leader movement on the left is out of symmetry with the one on the right.

Dan: There's a good reason for that, Frank. The leader of that line is freshman redshirt, James "Big Bone"

Culverhouse, an alternate who just yesterday replaced Slide Sullivan, who was injured in a football game with other band members.

Al: Even with the alignment problems, it's a very entertaining feature.

Frank: The elephant costumes the bass drummers are wearing add a creative flair.

Dan: I still haven't figured out how they hit the drums with those trunks.

Al: Well, that's it for the second number and there's a great response from the crowd. Now it's on to their production number, "Themes from Dumbo."

Dan: I think this is where the majorettes get to come up front.

Frank: What do you know about the Pachyderm majorette line, Dan?

Dan: I was talking to Polly Poise, the majorette sponsor, and she said all six members of the majorette squad completed 85 percent of their baton passes.

Frank: I know some NFL quarterbacks who'd take 85 percent.

Dan: The line is trying some difficult moves tonight. At one point they will throw the batons thirty yards into the air.

Al: It looks like they're lining up on opposite sides of the fifty to attempt it now. There goes the first toss!

Frank: OOPS!

Al: Second toss!

Frank: OOPS!

Al: They really need this one! It's a real Hail Mary! Third toss!

Dan: What a catch!

Al: That was Suzie Suregrip, the best twirler on the squad and still only a sophomore.

Frank: Let's watch that catch in slow motion.

Dan: Notice the perfect trajectory on that pass from Josie Montana. It arched beautifully over all ten sousaphone bells.

Frank: Notice the concentration as Suzie extends her body fully to catch the baton.

Al: Let's turn now to the flag line as the band climaxes this medley with "Pachyderms on Parade."

Dan: What are they doing down there?

Frank: It looks like they are pulling something from behind a screen placed on the fifty yard line.

Dan: It's an inflatable elephant, and they're filling it up with helium!

Al: The fans are going wild! That thing must be forty feet high!

Dan: What a climax! How will they ever top this with their closer?

Frank: I guess we'll see now as the band begins their customized arrangement of Camille Saint-Saens' "The Elephant" from his famous *The Carnival of the Animals*. It looks like the band is going to open with a flute and tuba duet.

Dan: That's not really a flute, Al. I think it's called a piccolo.

Al: You're right, Dan. My error. This is a rather unusual beginning.

Frank: The tune sounds rather familiar.

Monday Night Football

Dan: That's because the melody is actually borrowed from Berlioz's *La damnation de Faust*.

Frank: From the "Ballet des sylphes"?

Dan: Right.

Al: That tuba player, Lips Larson, is sure to be an All-State player this year.

Frank: He moves real good for a big man.

Dan: We have another problem on the right. Someone has tripped on the turf and started a domino effect in the clarinet section.

Frank: I talked with some of the students yesterday, and they seem to prefer natural grass because they sustain fewer injuries on that surface.

Al: Things are looking bad for the band right now. How are they going to recover from that terrible mistake?

Dan: The only thing that can save them now is — yes — here it comes!

Al: I see it coming too! It's a —

All three: COMPANY FRONT!

Al: What a sound!

Frank: What power from those brasses!

Dan: Look at those straight lines!

Frank: What intonation!

Al: The crowd is going wild!

Dan: What a dismount by the drum major!

Frank: I give him a perfect 10!

Al: That's a closer we won't soon forget!

Dan: The band parents have just dumped a twenty-gallon container of Gatorade on the director's head!

Al: We'll be back with a recap after these messages.

Dear Santa

As Christmas approaches, my thoughts can't help but turn to what I would like to see under the Christmas tree. While others may be dreaming of a white Christmas, I dream of gifts that have an odd, yet understandable, similarity to one another—they reduce stress. I've always believed that it would be some seemingly insignificant matter that sends me over the edge into a world of insanity. Maybe if I received that perfect gift for Christmas, I could reduce that possibility.

For instance, I would give almost anything for the **Tuba Permahandle**, a tuba case handle that doesn't break off within five weeks of purchase. Most of the tuba cases in my bandroom are jury-rigged with coat hangers and duct tape. The others have no handles, so students carry them over their heads and look like servants in old Tarzan movies, traipsing through the jungle with luggage on their heads.

I also need a gift that will help me find things. The **Acme Eraser and Chalk Tracker** would be great. Though I suspect that my chalk is primarily wasted by flute players who write a record of their love lives on the blackboard (Susie Loves Billy, etc.), there is still a certain mysteriousness about how chalk disappears and is *never* there when you need it. (And it is always in the chalk tray when you *don't* need it—just like the eraser.) The Acme Eraser and Chalk tracker has small electronic strips that attach to the eraser and chalk and will emit sound when you press a button on your special keychain. These same electronic strips can be added to percussion equipment. I am sick of losing percussion equipment, however small. I believe these items end up in two places: the same black hole that socks go after being thrown in the dryer or in the home of some human pack rat. I wouldn't be surprised if I read in the newspaper someday about some former band member who died and left 3,000 mallets to posterity, none of which match. (He would be the same person with 5,000 band books under his bed that were stolen from hapless beginners.) When percussion items are taken from the bandroom, the electronic strips would trigger a 1,000 decibel rendering of the Barney song.

Another perfect gift would be the **Nerf Baton**. Imagine the stress I could relieve by tossing one of those across the room without the fear of injuring anyone with flying fiberglass.

What would Christmas be without receiving some type of personal hygiene product? Instead of the more traditional cologne, I could use **Thick Skin Cream**. This transparent cream with a slight scent of citrus valve oil will enable me to withstand the criticisms of irate parents and disgruntled administrators.

Or how about something to help me with my traditional (yet perennially unsuccessful) New Year's resolution to lose weight? **Flesh-Toned Duct Tape** could be the answer. I could apply a strip or two under my chin, stretch it behind my neck and reduce my chins by one or two. A little tape around the waist could move everything back and up. This would enable me to fulfill my obligation of faithfully supporting the band concession stand and eating leftover fundraising candy.

I might even like to receive something to pass on to my students. **Quit-No-More** would be great. It's a mind-altering vitamin (shaped like John Philip Sousa, Henry Fillmore, or other famous bandmasters) that develops commitment and dependability in students. The **Smart Hat** would help poor marchers. Mini-speakers inside the hat boom "left-right" throughout the duration of a halftime show. **The Key Signature Shock Device** attaches to any instrument and provides a very slight shock to the fingertips when the wrong key signature is played.

A gift to reduce noise levels would also be ideal. Just the thought of the **Econo Oboe Mute** relaxes me, although I could just as easily settle for an oboe reed that requires no adjustments whatsoever and could withstand being run over by a pickup truck.

I know teachers love their students, but there are times when they just need to be alone. Thirty minutes before a concert when three hundred parasitic beginners are following me around like mosquitoes, some **Student-Be-Gone Repellent** would give me time to think. Harmless to students, Student-Be-Gone makes them avoid their director without knowing why.

I would really like a **Virtual Reality Band Trip.** I could give each band member special glasses, and we would all take off for anywhere in the world. This would save bus and hotel costs, and we would never have to leave the bandroom.

I suppose, however, that the ultimate Christmas gift would be a **scrolled budget written in the finest**

calligraphy and especially gift wrapped by our superintendent. Under the amount given, there would be a fill-in-the-blank where I could write in any amount desired.

Unfortunately, none of these gifts have been invented yet. I expect to receive an unlimited budget about the same time as the company car. Until then I'll have to be satisfied with aftershave, ties, flannel shirts, socks, and underwear.

The Fine Art of Publicity

There's an old joke from the Cold War about a sports story in the Soviet newspaper *Pravda* that reports the results of a car race between the Soviets and the Americans. The American race car won the duel so the *Pravda* headline read: SOVIET RACER COMES IN SECOND, AMERICAN RACER SECOND TO LAST. What the Soviets knew, before American politicians turned it into an art form, was the importance of spin.

Parents love to see their little Kenny G in the local paper, and every superintendent loves the attention it draws to the school district, so putting just the right spin on a band story can be the difference between a mundane announcement and an earth-shattering proclamation. In the examples below, you will see that it only takes a little clever adjustment to make a rather dull headline into an exciting one that will have those locals in a banner-waving frenzy. Don't worry about the accuracy of particular details; they only get in the way of a nice story.

Dull
The Pittsville Marching Pachyderms received a third division rating at Region Contest on Saturday, October 17.

Exciting
The Pittsville Marching Pachyderms placed third at the prestigious Region VIII Marching Festival where more than thirty bands participated. It was the highest placement for the band in twenty years.

You can see in the example above that a mere third division becomes third place (no use quibbling over details). It also helps to add how many bands participated (if this works to your advantage) and compare it to the bands of your school's past before you were the director.

Dull
The Glendale Marching Gladiolas placed second in their class at the Bands of the Northern Hemisphere competition in Dallas, Texas.

Exciting

The Glendale Marching Gladiolas placed second in their class and scored higher than any other band from the four-state area of Arkansas, Texas, Louisiana, and Oklahoma at the Bands of the Northern Hemisphere competition in Dallas, Texas.

It doesn't matter that there were no bands from those states at the competition.

Dull

The Bridgetown Marching Beavers were awarded fourth place at the American Celebration Music Festival in Concord, Massachusetts.

Exciting

The Bridgetown Marching Beavers placed fourth *in the nation* at the American Celebration of Music Festival in Concord, Massachusetts.

It was a national contest. Nevermind only five bands showed up.

Dull
The Canfield Marching Celeryfeds have been invited to perform in Washington, D.C. for the celebration of the 150-year anniversary of Washington's crossing of the Delaware.

Exciting
The Canfield Marching Celeryfeds have been invited to perform in Washington, D.C. for the celebration of the 150-year anniversary of Washington's crossing of the Delaware. They are the only Florida band invited to attend this historic event and were selected based on their prestigious and long-standing reputation.

It is important to point out, if possible, that you are the only band to do something. Use as wide a geographical area as possible. It matters little that you were the only band willing to pay the $400,000 it took to attend.

Dull
The Schwartzcof Marching Howitzers won many awards last Saturday at the Northern South Central South Dakota Regional Marching Championships.

Exciting

The Schwartzcof Marching Howitzers swept all the awards last Saturday at the Northern South Central South Dakota Regional Marching Championships. Superior ratings were received by the Howitzer flag line, majorettes, drum major, trombone soloist, trumpet soloist, woodwind quintet, and pit crew. Best in the Silver Class Awards (which are harder to get than those in the Bronze Class) went to the percussion line, brass line, and feature twirler. The Louis "Satchmo" Armstrong Jazziest Solo Honorable Mention went to trumpet player Lips McClelland in the 3A Amateur Division of the Blue Class (the second largest class next to the Gold Class). The Howitzers placed first in Class C of the Silver Division and had a higher score than all bands whose school name begins with the letter S. The band's score of 90.8754921 in the Overall Effect category was the second highest total (only .000001 behind the winner) of any band, regardless of class, division, sex, religion, or ethnic origin.

This write-up is particularly effective because the local readers get overwhelmed and confused, but are bound to conclude that their town has a doggone good band. The word "swept" is a nice term denoting total domination of the event.

Dull

The Boony Rapids Marching Mayflies placed in the top ten at the Bands of Distinction Marching Championships in LeBlanc, Wisconsin.

Exciting

The Boony Rapids Marching Mayflies were the only band from a school with a student population of under 250, no central heat and air, a band budget under $1,000, a band director with a badly receding hairline, and an average student ACT score of under 9 to place in the top ten at the thirtieth annual Bands of Distinction Marching Championships in LeBlanc, Wisconsin.

Stating the obstacles your band had to overcome to succeed at a contest builds sympathy and amazement at the same time.

The above examples are just a sampling of what can be done if you apply a little creativity. Make a few changes here and there to a mundane headline and you can spin your way to a band that proves the adage "image is everything."

Disclaimer: The above article was written with tongue in cheek (which is not easy for extended periods of time). Some of the techniques described above can be used as legitimate and ethical spin. However, if there were any you considered rather unsavory, assume I was kidding.

Ready or Not— Your Final Test

So here you are—a first year teacher. You have completed your formal education and are about to be thrust into the real world. Just to make sure you are ready, I have prepared a final exam.

1. School begins. When is the first time you should smile?

    A.   December.
    B.   Your third year of teaching.
    C.   The first time you hear the band play.
    D.   The first time you meet a student.

Answer: D should work just fine.

2. A student repeatedly commits small, but nagging annoyances that disrupt the class. What action should you take?

    A.   Tell him that you will cut off a finger each time he repeats an offense and follow through.
    B.   If he's a drummer, there's nothing you can do. Learn to accept it.
    C.   Assume he has some medical condition that prevents him from behaving. Your continued suffering will make you feel more a part of the teaching community.
    D.   Set clear, firm, reasonable limits for the student. Meet with parents if necessary.

Answer: D- It is important that you have a definite discipline plan that is approved and supported by your administration. Unless your principal is Attila the Hun, answer A will not be approved, though the thought of it may be rather pleasing. Meeting with parents can often work wonders — I could kick myself for the times I put it off too long.

3. You realize two weeks before concert contest that the music you have chosen is too difficult for your band. What do you do?

> A. Schedule four-hour rehearsals every day after school until contest.
> B. Immediately change to easier music.
> C. Take your chances and then blame the kids for not practicing enough and the judges for not giving you credit for playing tough music.
> D. Don't attend the contest.

Answer: There is no easy answer to this one. Preparation is the key to avoiding this situation altogether, but if you had to choose one, the best answer may be a combination of A and B. Admit to the kids your mistake, give out easier music and practice a reasonable amount after school.

4. Which of the following is the *most* important to have a good relationship with?

> A. Custodian
> B. Lunch ladies
> C. Principal
> D. Band parents
> E. Superintendent

Answer: I guess the answer to this one depends on your priorities. A if you want a clean room and first dibs on school gossip, B if you like a little extra dessert on your plate, C if you want anything, D if you don't want to run the concession stand by yourself, or E if you want to keep your job. To be safe, you'd better get along with all of them.

5. Irrational parents go ballistic and insult your whole family tree because their kid did not get first chair. What should you do?

    A.   Tell them to put their kid in another school if they're not happy.

    B.   Tell them their kid has about as much talent as a piece of salami, and it would be better if the kid switched to underwater basket weaving class.

    C.   Ask them to step outside for a little mano a mano "discussion."

    D.   The more upset they get, the more calm you should get. Explain your position. If things get too confrontational, stop the discussion and reschedule the meeting for a time when the principal can be present.

Answer: D is best. It may be helpful to admit that chair placement is subjective to a degree and that part of your job is to make the tough decisions. Try to maintain an encouraging tone and state your commitment to helping the student become the best player he or she can be, regardless of chair. Stress the concept of teamwork and the importance of all players.

6. A student asks, "How old are you?" How do you respond?

  A. "None of your business."
  B. "Sixty-five. I had a hard time with third grade."
  C. With the truth.
  D. "Thirty-nine."

Answer: It doesn't really matter because most kids will think you are too old while their parents think you are too young. D is a good answer because you will probably use it from 40 years on anyway.

7. It's time for your first fundraising venture. What do you sell?

  A. The first thing a fundraising salesman brings to your office.
  B. Whatever the band has sold the last twenty years before your arrival.

C. It doesn't matter as long as there are good prizes.
D. Whatever the band boosters want.

Answer: A is a little hasty—meet with the inevitable twenty or more who visit you your first year. (Pick one who supports bands by purchasing booth space at conventions.) B may be smart if the stuff sells. C is often true, but you can do better. D can be great. If they will do the work, let them have it and you teach.

8. You want to do something, but you are afraid the principal will say no. What is your course of action?

A. Do what you want and ask for forgiveness later.
B. Ask him anyway.
C. Ask the assistant principal and hope he says it is okay. If he says no, then go to the principal.
D. Don't take any initiative your first year; it's bound to fail.

Answer: This is a tough one. Your first year it is better to try B (maybe you'll luck out and he will be reasonable). If this fails the first time or two, you may try A, though C is safer.

9. A second year trumpet player fingers B♭ with the second valve for the hundredth time in a week. What would be your wisest move?

    A.   Ask him if his mother drank alcohol while she was pregnant.
    B.   Send him to the football coach with a high recommendation.
    C.   Make sure the student is actually reading music (not just associating fingerings with the place of a note on the staff). Review note names and meaning of key signatures.
    D.   Have him write "B♭ is first valve" one hundred times on the blackboard or a sheet of paper.

Answer: A is mean, but smart aleck questions bring a unique sense of relief. C is a kinder and gentler response. If this doesn't work, try D—pure rote might be your only answer.

10. It is your first teachers' meeting. What do you do?

   A. Sit in the dark, remote recesses of the room with the coaches and read the sports section when they are finished.
   B. Skip it for a band rehearsal.
   C. Sit on the front row and take notes, asking pertinent questions as sincerely as possible.
   D. Read a copy of *The Instrumentalist* that you have placed just to the side of the meeting's printed agenda.

Answer: Save A for closer to your retirement years—you will have heard it all by then. B might work once. C might be good if your principal can't recognize an act when he sees one. D is a far more profitable way to spend your time.

11. Your first chair trumpet player wants to quit band at the end of the year. What do you do?

   A. Fall to the ground with hands clasped and beg him to reconsider.
   B. Tell him he can't quit—he's fired.
   C. Have a conference with the student and/or parents.
   D. Wish him luck and encourage him to rejoin in the future.

Answer: Avoid answer B. It's very easy to be defensive in such situations and write a kid off very quickly, but if the student has not been a troublemaker and has made positive contributions to the band, it may be worth the effort to keep him in. It's important not to burn bridges in these situations. The student may come to his senses later (he is just a kid after all) or he may have a younger brother or sister you want in your band in the future. The best answer is probably some combination of C and D.

12. A student says, "Our director last year, Mr. Thimblestop, never did it that way." How should you respond?

    A.   "Mr. Thimblestop was an idiot."
    B.   "I am your director now. I am your mama. I am your daddy. I am your whole family tree." (Add a maniacal laugh at the end.)
    C.   "That's why the band sounded like crud."
    D.   "There is more than one way to do things. Let's try it this way and see what happens."

Answer: D is best.

13. The football coach makes several disparaging remarks about the band to students in PE class. You should—

    A.   Play "Looney Tunes" in the stands the next time the football team is getting stomped.
    B.   Tell the kids the coach took one hit too many in college.
    C.   Play "Iron Man" at *ffffff* while your team has the ball.
    D.   Talk to the coach to clear the air.
    E.   Ignore the problem.

Answer: Fighting this problem might not be worth the effort. If you choose D, remember to be kind—three losing seasons and this guy may be your principal.

14. Football team members send you a petition asking that the band play more tunes that will fire them up. You should—

   A.   Send the coach a petition listing plays the band wants the offense to run.
   B.   Don't play anything in the stands the next game.
   C.   Go on like always.
   D.   Play John Tesh and Yanni arrangements at the next football game.

Answer: No use being obnoxious, choose C.

15. The cheerleaders keep requesting that the band play their favorite song (and you are sick of the song). Now what?

   A.   Gradually speed up your fight song until the cheerleaders are spinning out of control.
   B.   Begin drum cadences in the middle of their chants.
   C.   Scream "DO I LOOK LIKE A DJ OR SOMETHING?"
   D.   Play the stupid song.

Answer: D. Play the stupid song. It will make their day.

16. The band boosters want to use fundraising money to take the band on a trip to the Inner Mongolia Winter Parade. You want instruments. How do you approach this?

    A.   Go to Inner Mongolia.
    B.   Compromise on a closer trip (like Outer Mongolia).
    C.   Point out specific needs of the program and the musical benefit it will be for their kids.
    D.   Promise a bigger trip when the band has met more of its pressing needs.

Answer: Some combination of B, C, and D would be best. If they are violently adamant, go to Inner Mongolia—they earned the money.

17. The drama teacher has nailed the set for their spring play to the stage floor and your concert is two days before the opening night of the play. What do you do?

    A.   Run to the principal and whine.
    B.   Get some low brass players, several hammers and start rippin' nails.

C. Next time you direct the orchestra for the spring musical, push the dynamics up so high that no one can hear the singers.
D. Talk to the drama teacher first. Work out a compromise and be willing to help take down and put up all or portions of a set.
E. Find an alternate site for the concert and start reserving the stage ten years in advance.

Answer: Early communication may have prevented this, but things happen. Try to work something out before going to the principal. It's bad for a principal to have to mediate for fellow members of the arts (even if those drama folks are a little quirky). D and E are the best choices.

18. A freshman does not show for a Friday night game and the absence is unexcused. What is the best course of action?

A. Have a schedule change slip waiting for him Monday.
B. Hold a parent conference to determine his future status.
C. Toilet paper his yard that night.

D. Chew him out in front of the band on Monday.

Answer: B is generally best. I find that most kids who miss a performance never seem to really "get it" and cause problems later on. On the other hand, I have had just enough freshmen mature and develop into dependable young people to give the kid a second chance after a parent conference. Make sure your policies are clear to the students and parents before the season starts and have rules that allow for some flexibility.

19. Which of the following phrases would be best avoided?

   A. "When I was in band . . . "
   B. "Uh . . . uh . . . uh . . . uh . . . "
   C. "You know . . . . you know . . . ."
   D. "Shhhh . . . blah blah blah . . . Shhhhh. . . . . blah, blah, blah"
   E. To a principal: "I assumed that . . . "
   F. All of the above.

Answer: F is the best answer. (Principals will really jump on "I assumed . . . ")

20. Your band students win several awards at a contest. What should you do next?

      A.   Put their picture in the paper as soon as possible.
      B.   Put their names in the school announcements.
      C.   Put their names and/or pictures on the school or local television channel.
      D.   All of the above

Answer: D. Image is everything.

21. A kid says, "Everybody is quitting next year." What should you say?

      A.   "So am I—so there!"
      B.   "Those who want to have a great band and be a part of something big will stay. If anyone quits, it will be their loss."
      C.   "I hope *you* are, loser."
      D.   "Who made you spokesperson for the people?"

Answer: B is the most diplomatic.

22. A beginner says he cannot come to the concert because he is playing in a little league baseball game. His dad is the coach. What do you do?

   A. Kick the rascal out.
   B. Give him an "F" for his concert grade, but let him stay in.
   C. Excuse the absence and have him write a make-up report.
   D. Move the concert date.

Answer: Clearing the date far ahead of time will alleviate most scheduling problems. Some, however, are unavoidable. Check with principal before making a decision. There is no easy answer on this one. Fail the kid and he may quit. Excuse him and you have to excuse everyone else's reasons also. C is probably in the best interest of the kid—he didn't schedule the game or the concert.

23. At the first parent/teacher conference a parent asks how his child is doing. The kid has absolutely no ability, but he loves band. What do you say?

   A. "Wonderful. He's such a nice kid."
   B. "He has a problem with rhythm, pitches, tonguing, and tone, but other than that he is doing fine."

C. "He's having some major problems right now, but we will continue to work with him to bring out his full potential. If he does not make much progress over the next couple of months, I will call you to decide the best course of action."
D. "Has he ever tried choir?"

Answer: Something like C is best. Frankness is very important, particularly if the parents are making monthly payments on a new instrument. Work hard to find some role for that kid in your band.

24. A student points out in front of the class that your zipper is down. What do you do?

A. Ignore him and move on.
B. Look down and check.
C. Run to the teachers' lounge.
D. Turn around and dramatically pull it up.

Answer: I like answer D. There's nothing like a little humor to defuse an embarrassing situation—might as well make it memorable while you're at it.

25. The principal asks you to play Elvis in the school lip-sync contest. What do you say?

    A.   "Thank you, thank you very much, but no."
    B.   "I have a death in the family that day."
    C.   "I don't look good in sideburns."
    D.   "That would be fun. I've always thought of myself as a hunka-hunka burnin' love."

Answer: D is the best answer. Your kids would enjoy seeing you loosen up a little.

Hopefully this quiz will help you anticipate some future situations that you may find yourself in. Best of luck as your *real* test begins.

Lots of Wind from PDQ Bach

It is a fair question to ask why anyone would do an interpretive analysis of *Grand Serenade for an Awful Lot of Winds and Percussion.* A better question is why anyone would write the work in the first place. In *The Definitive Biography of P.D.Q. Bach,* Peter Schickele points out that P.D.Q. Bach's music has a therapeutic effect on audiences. Whereas the music of Mozart and Bach might give listeners an inferiority complex because they could never approach such beauty themselves, the music of P.D.Q. Bach leaves a comforting feeling that even without music lessons they could have written something just as good.

In the program notes, Professor Schickele warns the director not to try to realize the composer's intentions because doing so would be a waste of time since he probably didn't have any. Despite this, I believe an interpretive analysis would be a worthy pursuit. What greater challenge could there be than to interpret a work with no meaning?

Composed originally for Prince Fred of Wein-am-Rein for some kind of outdoor occasion (my guess is a garage sale), *Grand Serenade* consists of four movements, each movement a little more disturbing than the preceding one, in what is best described as a growing musical avalanche that threatens to consume all who encounter it.

The first movement, "Grand Entrance," has a marked tempo of ♩ = 88 beats per minute. I have found a slightly faster tempo more effective since it gets the movement over with sooner. The first trumpet part in measure one reaches a high C. If your trumpet players cannot play this, give it to a muted oboe. At boxed(A), you may want to have players insert earplugs to avoid any possible lawsuits filed because of the high G in the

clarinet part. At measure 11, the score indicates a duck call the first time and a car horn or gun shot the second time. For proper duck call techniques, students should study such reference works as *Billy Bob's Guide to 1001 Duck Calls* (published by Ducks Are Us) or *Duck Calls for Dummies*. Be sure the gun is loaded with blanks and pointed upward. At the premiere performance, the percussionist accidentally aimed a gun loaded with live ammunition forward and, unfortunately, missed P.D.Q. by a couple of inches. The entire account is recorded in the article "18th-Century Weaponry and P.D.Q. Bach— What Went Wrong?" in the January 1997 *Journal of the National Firearms Association*.

The second movement, "Simply Grand Minuet," is unusual for P.D.Q. minuets because it is in $\frac{3}{4}$ time. The piece begins with horns in octaves on a concert $B\flat$, a

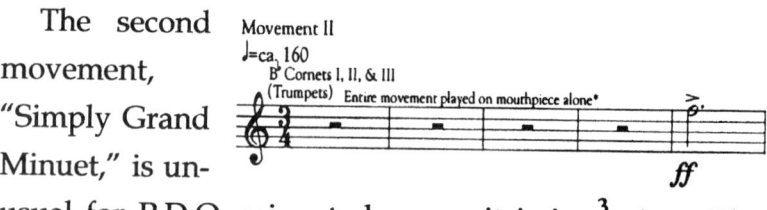

rather unreasonable expectation and a sign of early dementia in P.D.Q. One unique feature is its use of mouthpiece buzzing in the trumpet section. This is a good idea, not necessarily for musical reasons but because it is probably the only time trumpet players will buzz their mouthpieces despite repeated suggestions over the years by their teachers to do so. Consider eliminating the repeats to spare the audience further agony and to reduce the spittle falling on the woodwind section. The low $B♭$ s in the trombone parts at measure 9 show P.D.Q.'s programmatic skills and the influence of alcohol on his writing ability as he attempts to imitate sounds that drinking can cause. See *The Biographical Dictionary of Demented Musicians and Composers* (Vol. 18) for other examples of this disgusting practice.

The chromatic scale at $\boxed{C}$ shows the influence of Belwin's venerable First Division

Band Method. Measures 19-20 show P.D.Q.'s uncanny ability to write for instruments that had not been invented yet. If the piccolo duet cannot be played in tune, hide the second chair player's instrument.

At measure 36, the clarinets gargle water. It might be a good idea to have your students obtain permission slips. Two clarinet players from a small band in South Dakota drowned while performing this measure.

"Romance in the Grand Manner," the third movement, introduces a hauntingly appropriate theme. Appropriate because it was lifted from fellow alcoholic Stephen Foster who lived some years after P.D.Q.'s death. Some musicologists defend P.D.Q. saying that the similarities in their music are simply due to the effects that alcohol had on their creative processes. See "P.D.Q. Bach and Alcoholism—Did It Help or Hurt?" in the September 1998 issue of the *Procrastinator's Quarterly* that is due out some time next year (or the year after). It is no coincidence that the only instrument on which P.D.Q. was an acknowledged virtuoso was the wine bottle. The theme requires a good French horn player; for added effect, have a lousy one play it.

At A , the trombones and baritones have ⌢̈, notation most composers use to indicate a specific articulation. P.D.Q. probably just couldn't make up his mind. In other manuscripts he used the following markings:

In the last measure there are two notes for oboe. If you are lucky enough to have only one oboe player, the player should play the top notes since they will probably be so flat that the lower pitch is the one that actually sounds. If you don't have any oboes . . . congratulations!

The fourth movement, "Rondo Mucho Grando," begins with long timpani rolls and undampened cymbal crashes. The director is encouraged to be as dramatic as possible because the music needs all the help it can get. I suggest having a guest performer, such as a school administrator, play the cymbals. Measure 6 requires the cymbal player to drop the cymbals. Make sure to caution the percussion section not to drop any cymbals (as is their custom) prior to this movement.

The police whistle in measure 14 should be blown with lots of air. If you do not own a police whistle, ask one of your percussionists to borrow one the next time he is down at the local jail.

Both ⎡F⎤ and ⎡G⎤ show that P.D.Q. had some knowledge of scales (just make sure your clarinet and trumpet soloists do also).

The march that begins at ⎡L⎤ was possibly stolen from Wiener Schnitzel University. It is believed to be the fight song played for the university's bratwurst tossing team. See the book *Obscure Fight Songs of 18th-Century German Universities* by Victor S. Marsch.

In the first ending after ⎡U⎤ (measure 192), I have found it very effective to substitute a grunt (a forceful "UHH") for the note in the chimes. It adds a primeval touch that is most appealing.

The piece ends with an opportunity for eight different percussionists to perform as soloists. I know this is rather frightful, but it will make their year. The bass drum solo in measure 234 is marked *fff*, so ask the bass drummer to bring the dynamic down from his normal *fffff*.

First published in 1975, *Grand Serenade* is amazingly still in print. As Schickele points out, perform the music well, so that if the inevitable critical backlash develops, the performing ensemble can justly claim that it wasn't their fault.

Granddaddy's Baton

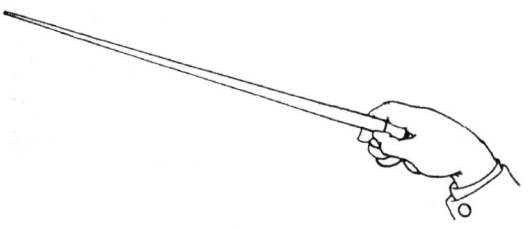

My grandfather loved music. His evenings were often spent sitting in his trusty, worn recliner watching orchestral concerts on public television broadcasts. As the sound of the orchestra filled the room, he would view performances with the same vigilance other men would expend in watching a Super Bowl. The various conductors were his coaches, the performers his athletes, and the music his gridiron. His arms would conduct in graceful motions as the music flowed like a halfback running in slow-motion. As the music gained intensity, his conducting would become more like a 250 pound fullback crashing through a defensive line.

My grandfather was a distinguished band director for over thirty years. My mother had been a fine clarinet player in his band and continued her music studies at the collegiate level where she became a member of the Florida State University marching band and met my father. Consequently, when I reached sixth grade, it was with a special measure of pride that I joined the band program, for I was continuing a family tradition.

Though separated by many miles over the years from growing up in a military family, I would ask Granddaddy for lessons on our visits to his Florida home each Christmas. He would guide me through my Arban book, a trusty inch-thick text full of musical exercises for trumpet written by the famous nineteenth-century cornetist, Jean-Baptiste Arban.

From time to time, Granddaddy would come to our home for a visit. One year I was particularly excited because he was going to be able to attend one of my concerts. After it was over, an odd absence of encouragement followed. I waited expectantly for compliments that were not forthcoming. I was not really sure what to make of this. Did he not think my band was any good? Did he not think *I* was any good?

As I grew older, my interest in music grew to the point that by my junior year in high school I knew I wanted to be a band director. I even wrote a term paper on how to build a successful band program. My parents were very supportive of this decision, but I expected special interest from Granddaddy regarding my career choice. If I had chosen some other career, I suppose it would not have seemed as important to have Granddaddy's approval.

I slowly began to discover that my grandfather had an inexplicable inability to show a keen interest in my musical development. After I entered college as a music major, conversations I would initiate with him about band directing were short-lived and of little substance.

After graduating from college in 1985, I began teaching junior high school band in Paragould, a small Arkansas town two hours north of where my parents had settled after retiring from the military. My mother brought Granddaddy to see me, and I was excited and proud to have him at my band concert during his visit. I knew the band wasn't the best he would have ever heard, but I was enough of a musician to know that the group merited some praise, however faint it might be. After the concert, family members complimented the program. My parents were particularly proud. But again, there was an unsettling silence from the one whose blessing could mean the most.

It was at that point that I gave up on ever pleasing him. At least I thought so at the time. When Granddaddy had a stroke in 1987, a sadness came over me as I came to the realization that with his new health problems I was unlikely to ever gain the encouragement I sought. Granddaddy continued teaching clarinet lessons to area students as he had since his retirement, but he found it too difficult to talk understandably, and he soon had to quit. On one visit to our home, he painstakingly communicated to me in hand gestures that although he could still play various melodies on his clarinet, he could not read music anymore, nor did he really know what he was playing.

Our visits together were sporadic until he died of lung cancer in May of 1995. After several days of sorting his belongings my mother brought me two items—his clarinet and a baton with his initials on it. Despite my inner denials, I was hoping that he had purposefully set these things aside for me, a last-minute chance that despite his medical condition he had given me some sign of his blessing. Unfortunately, this was not the case. They were simply left behind with his other belongings, and my mother thought I might like to have them.

Granddaddy's Baton

The clarinet was badly in need of repair from years of neglect, having been abandoned in frustration years before. The smooth, wooden baton was eighteen inches long, much longer than most band directors use today. Near the baton's base, Granddaddy's name was inscribed on a silver band. A familiar regretfulness surfaced as I set the baton on one of my bookshelves, uncertain as to my feelings about it.

Almost three years passed before I picked the baton up again. One evening as I was preparing for a rehearsal to be held the next day, I was looking over Gustav Holst's *Second Suite in F*, a famous four-movement band work of ultimate musical craftsmanship. While looking over the pages of the musical score and listening to a recording on my stereo, I couldn't help but conduct along with "Song of the Blacksmith," a movement that requires a very precise conducting pattern for complete clarity. Wanting more precision than just my hand could provide, I glanced around, looking for a baton. I saw Granddaddy's baton up on the shelf, reached for it, and slowly brought it down.

I started the recording again and as I conducted, bitterness clawed its way through the exciting forces of the music. At the conclusion of the music, I sat motionless for several minutes. What was I feeling exactly? My mind was a jumbled concerto, the notes flying randomly from bar to bar. Why didn't Granddaddy encourage me? Is there any way to end the bitterness I feel? Is it really that important? I have great parents and a great family of my own. I'm a secure person. Why worry about it?

I couldn't talk myself out of resolving the issue. Over the next few months, I wrestled with my feelings, much like Beethoven struggled to complete symphonies, encumbered by hearing loss and its accompanying frustrations. I used Granddaddy's baton many times as I rehearsed at home. It became clear to me that the answer might lie in music. Just as music formed a separation between us, it seemed likely to be the force that could bring us back together.

I began to realize that our relationship was one of parallel love. Our love of music, the excitement of conducting, and the thrill of guiding young people to heights they never thought possible were things we shared whether we spoke of them or not. Although this love never fully intersected the way I had hoped, there was comfort in the fact that we derived much of our joy in life the same way.

I also realized that just as music can be loved and enjoyed without full understanding, so too can people. One need not understand every aspect of

Granddaddy's Baton

musical composition to find excitement in a great musical work. The great musical lines penned by master composers convey a beauty that can be enjoyed by the least experienced of novices and the greatest of musicologists alike. In the same way, I don't need to fully understand Granddaddy to appreciate him. I *can* have love without understanding.

It's interesting that Granddaddy's baton brought us together in a way that he, for whatever reason, could not. I am at peace with Granddaddy now and use his baton as I study my music for rehearsals. One of the most beloved symphonies ever written is Franz Schubert's *Symphony No. 8 in B minor*, more popularly known as the *Unfinished Symphony*. The symphony, mysteriously left by Schubert with only two of the four movements completed, is a lyrical, passionate work of undying beauty that has left listeners with a completely satisfying musical experience despite its unfinished state.

In a way I am conducting my own unfinished symphony—and as Schubert has proven, even unfinished symphonies can be beautiful.

Fables in 4/4 Time

James Thurber (1894-1961) was one of the greatest humorists of all time. His book, *Fables for Our Time*, is a collection of stories with humorous and off-the-wall morals. Without any pretense of being the next James Thurber, I present some fables from an educational perspective.

The Rabbit Who Knew Too Much

There once was a rabbit who got up one morning and decided to leave his home in the field to find one up in the hills. Early that evening, after hunting for a good spot all day in the hot sun, the rabbit came to a hill where there were many empty rabbit holes. "This is great! I will not even have to dig a hole in the ground—I can live in one of these," he assumed. Later that evening, just after the rabbit settled down for a good night's rest (for he was very tired from house-hunting) a snake came back home and ate the rabbit for supper.

Moral: When dealing with your principal, never assume anything.

The Monkey and the Lion

There once was a monkey who wanted to organize a coconut percussion ensemble for monkeys. So he went to the lion, the king of the jungle, to see if there was a time the ensemble could rehearse. When the lion looked at his master schedule, it looked as if he would have difficulty finding a time that would not conflict with the bird choir, the hyena laughing club, and the cheetah track club. The monkey suggested that they basically had three alternatives—disallow the class, schedule the class opposite the class with least conflicts, or add a new slot especially for the class. The lion told the monkey he would get back with him the next day and let him know his decision. Two weeks later (for time is relative with the king of the jungle) the monkey timidly approached the lion, after not hearing anything from him. The lion said that he decided to let the percussion ensemble meet at a time opposite the vine-swinging club, a required class for all monkeys.

Moral: After suggesting three good solutions to an administrator, he will devise a ludicrous or unproductive fourth.

The Father and the Son

There once was an old, egotistical elephant named Gabriel who could trumpet louder than anyone in the whole jungle. He never seemed to tire of blasting all day and all night and though all the animals of the jungle hated him, they had to admit he could really blow that trunk. One day the old elephant died, and his son Strad took over the job as chief trumpeter. Day and night he arrogantly strutted around blasting his trunk, but showing little of the talent and flair displayed by his father. It wasn't long before the animals of the jungle longed for the good old days when Gabriel was chief trumpeter.

Moral: The only thing worse than a trumpet player who thinks he is great and is, is one who thinks he is great, but isn't.

The Two Monkeys

There once were two monkeys who loved to play the drums and wanted to figure out a way to share their music with others. So they put their heads together and after several moments of deep thought came up with an idea. Why not perform for all the animals in the jungle to promote peace and understanding? So that's exactly what they did. They set up their little drums and began to play. Quite a crowd gathered to listen, but a lion broke up the concert and ate them both.

Moral #1: Two heads are not always better than one.

Moral #2: Some people just don't get it.

Moral #3: When planning a program, consider your audience.

The Chicken and the Farmer's Wife

There once was a little chicken who was smaller than the rest of the flock, so she decided to eat as much chicken feed as she could so that she would stop being pecked on. So every morning as the farmer's wife scattered seed around the coop the little chicken would quickly scurry and gobble up as much feed as she could. She ate so much during the next few weeks that she developed a very intimidating presence—so much so that no other chickens dared push her around. Then one day the farmer's wife looked down as she was scattering seed and said, "Oh my! What a nice, plump chicken! Perfect for Sunday dinner!"

Moral: When it comes to bands, bigger is not always better.

The Selfish Hyena

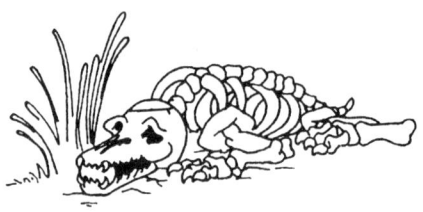

Once upon a time, there were three hyenas roaming around on the Serengeti looking for something to eat when, all of a sudden, the hyena named Slim looked down and saw a bright red ball lying in the grass. "Look what I found!" he exclaimed. But Bull, the largest hyena, snatched it with his powerful jaws and claimed it for his own. A big fight ensued, and Bull won the ball for himself after biting and clawing his friends until they ran away. Bull enjoyed having his newfound toy but other problems developed. All the other hyenas hated him, and he could not go hunt for food for fear that someone would steal his ball. So over a period of several weeks, Bull starved to death. He was found grasping his plastic ball.

Moral: Some things aren't worth fighting for.

The Tortoise and the Hare Conduct

Once upon a time there was a tortoise conductor and a hare conductor who were taking their bands to concert band contest. As their concluding number, both decided to perform Bernstein's *Candide*. The hare conducted the piece at a very quick tempo, but his band could not handle the piece technically. The tortoise conducted the piece very slowly, but precisely. When the final results were announced, a band won that did an easier piece both accurately and at the appropriate tempo.

Moral: #1: Slow and steady doesn't always make for an exciting performance.

Moral #2: Tortoises and hares should stick to foot races.

The Mind of the Wiseguy

Most band directors have at least one member of their band who would qualify as a bona fide wiseguy. This individual captures the hearts of fellow band members with his or her timely remarks and witticisms, often at the director's expense. Although the wiseguy's comments sometime provide a little comic relief to the rehearsal, they are usually timed so that all the director hears is a mumble and a ripple of snickers. Then the group members show a unity one wishes they would exhibit in their playing as they stare innocently into space. But everyone knows that the wiseguy has struck again, and the director cringes as the wiseguy cracks that silly smirk which seems to say, "You have no proof that I said anything!"

The Mind of the Wiseguy

Although there is no total cure for the wiseguy (with the exception of several illegal and violent options), band directors can learn to head off smart remarks by avoiding questions, clichés, and phrases which are so tempting to the opportunistic wiseguy. He is a formidable foe whose mind, though a little warped, is not void and formless but actually a fine-tuned machine ready to jump at the chance to display its quick wit and humor. The following suggestions should help you be on your guard.

Always try to avoid any reference to your age. Even young directors should realize that as soon as they begin teaching they have added thirty or forty years to their age in the minds of most kids. I made the mistake of telling a class about how disappointed I was as a senior in high school (1980) to unexpectedly receive a huge $200 clunker of a car from my parents (you could have fit the Mormon Tabernacle Choir in the back seat alone) when I was expecting something a little more appealing to girls in particular and mankind in general. One student (a closet wiseguy—I would have never expected it) raised her hand and asked, "But wasn't that a lot of money *back then?*"

It is just a matter of multiple-choice for the wiseguy when a disgruntled band director asks:

(1) "Do you think I was born yesterday?"

- A. "No, I'm not even sure you were born in this century."
- B. "I don't think so, but with as little hair as you have that could be a distinct possibility." (Wiseguys love to attack your physical make-up.)
- C. "I wonder if he wears Pampers or Huggies? (Wiseguys can be philosophical.)
- D. "That cliché is so old it doesn't even deserve a smart remark." (They can also be a little finicky.)

(2) "Just who do you think I am?"

- A. "Beats me." (Terse humor.)
- B. "I'm not sure but the face is familiar." (Probably a wiseguy who always has his head buried in the music.)
- C. "John Philip Sousa?" (At least it's related to music.)
- D. Several unprintable choices are also available.

(3) "Do you think I am some kind of idiot?"

- A. "Yes, without a doubt." (They can be blunt.)
- B. "Do you really want to know?"
- C. "The thought has crossed my mind."
- D. "No, I don't even think you're that smart." (Sometimes they have no mercy whatsoever.)

Wiseguys also have no problem adding clever comments to a director's examples and stories. They have little trouble supplying jokes for stories which begin with phrases like the following:

(1) "When I was a kid..."

- A. "*He* was a kid?"
- B. "They had kids *back then*?" (I've learned to despise those two words.)
- C. "I wonder if he knew Beethoven."
- D. "Oh, no, here comes his life story again." (Wiseguys have no appreciation of history.)

(2) "When *I* was in band . . ."

    A.   "They had bands *back then?*" (There they are again.)
    B.   "He was probably one of those teacher's pet/goody-two-shoes types."
    C.   "Was the saxophone invented yet?"
    D.   "Oh, no, here comes another one of his flashbacks."

Wiseguys also love to give the director's appearance a thorough check, so try to dress conservatively, yet with a little style. While it may be true that clothing styles run in cycles every fifteen or twenty years, it is not a good idea to bridge the gap by wearing the same style for twenty years. Try not to wear any clothes that are too trendy, particularly if they are made up of bright colors. Wiseguys have a whole stockpile of old jokes for bright clothes. "Hey, how many batteries does it take to keep those pants going?" and "Could you turn off your shirt? It's giving me a headache," are two examples. Be sure that whatever you wear matches perfectly. If you think you can get away with socks of slightly different shades, think again. Once a wiseguy notices, the word travels like wildfire and kids will be glancing at your ankles all day long. Don't wear white tube socks to avoid the problem (even if the stripes match)—things will probably get worse.

When handing out new music, avoid asking the band members' opinions of a new piece (if they haven't already volunteered it) before it has been played enough for an opinion to have some validity. The question "Do you like this piece?" can open a can of worms. The wiseguy, along with some part-timers (almost all the kids try to have their moments in the spotlight), will degrade the piece all the way from the composer's name to the music itself. Some even try renaming the piece to display their premature displeasure. I've had kids give certain works so many different names I even got confused. Some have fun musing on what they can do with the music: "Let's line my puppy's cage with it!" and the popular "Let's have a bonfire!" are two examples. Use what little dictatorial powers you have to stop things before a vote is taken.

"Hey, how many batteries does it take to keep those pants going?"

A final suggestion is to downplay farewells at various times of the year. It is so tempting to see if there is even the slightest chance that the kids might miss you when you are leaving for a clinic, convention, or such, but it is still best not to say something like "I'm going to be gone for the next couple of days. I hope you guys can manage without me." If you are expecting them to sadly chant, "What are we going to do?" think again. Before you have even finished the sentence the wiseguy already has the band doing the "wave" as they rejoice and sing "Happy Days Are Here Again" or its modern equivalent.

This is one instance when you can enjoy a small victory if, after the cheers and singing are over, you announce that Mrs. Battleaxe, the meanest substitute in the district (you innocently act like you had no idea she was the meanest), will be there in your place. Just watch their jubilation turn to utter humility as they grovel and beseech you not to leave. You are at the height of your popularity, so savor the moment.

I hope these suggestions have provided some guidelines in avoiding undue embarrassment. If you slip, just take the punches as good-naturedly as possible and remember them at the end of each grading period! Most importantly, learn to laugh at yourself and remember what a wiseguy you were as a kid.

My Fifteen Minutes of Fame in Reader's Digest

In March of 1997 I had a story published in the "Tales Out of School" department of *Reader's Digest* and experienced my "fifteen minutes of fame." How was the life of fame during those fifteen minutes? The following are some of the things that I experienced.

1. I became a local authority and consultant on magazine publishing. Everyone wanted to know how I did it. I also heard countless stories followed by the

inevitable, "Do you think *my* story is funny? Could it be published?"

2. I became a grief counselor, consoling people who came to me lamenting the fact that they had mailed *Reader's Digest* a story only to be rejected. I assured them it was nothing personal.

3. I also met hundreds of people who had been meaning to write their funny story, but just hadn't had the time. Some of them actually went ahead and sent their story in because of my good fortune. One of them was actually accepted.

4. Although I knew that *Reader's Digest* has a readership of about 27 million, I had never realized how many of my friends and acquaintances read it. I also found out that most of them read the funny departments first like I do.

5. I met slightly jealous individuals who would hint that my story wasn't that great and that they could do better.

6. I found that my finances came under good-natured scrutiny. "How much money did you make?"

seemed to be the most asked question. Many asked me what I was going to do with the money. People expected me to become an instant philanthropist. My preacher even told our church he expected my contributions to increase! (I made $400, if you must know.)

7. I received a letter from a man who saw my unusual name and wanted to know if we were related. We corresponded some, concluding that we were probably related, but nothing definite could be determined.

Many famous sports figures and entertainers decry the unseen horror of fame—the loss of privacy. Would I do it over again if I could? You bet. But I think I'll keep it fifteen minutes at a time. Here's the story that started it all:

One day I was showing the beginning band students at Ridgecrest Junior High School in Paragould, AR, the proper way to assemble and hold their instruments. "It is extremely important to connect the neck strap to the loop on the back of the instrument so it doesn't fall out of your hands at a careless moment," I explained. "Mr. Reely," a student in the back of the room quipped, "are you teaching us how to practice safe sax?"

Postscript: I have since tried to get other stories published in *Reader's Digest,* but it appears that I am but a flash in the old proverbial pan. Of course, my stories are much better than many I have seen published since 1997.

Classic Poetry Revisited

English was one of my favorite subjects in high school. This was due mainly to the fact that I had some fine teachers. I submit the following adaptations with apologies to these teachers as well as Longfellow, Keats, Tennyson, and Dickinson.

The Pitch Rises, the Pitch Falls
"The Tide Rises, the Tide Falls" by Henry Wadsworth Longfellow (1807-1882)

The pitch rises, the pitch falls,
The music softens, the oboe calls;
On concert stages of near perfection,
The cane reed mounts an insurrection,
    And the pitch rises, the pitch falls.

The music floats o'er concert halls,
But the flute, the flute in the altissimo calls;
The little note, that elusive dot,
Goes sharp when lips can't find their spot,
    And the pitch rises, the pitch falls.

The trombone rings; the tone center falls,
Then rises again as the director squalls;
The note returns, but nevermore
Returns the slide where it was before.
    And the pitch rises, the pitch falls.

Ode on a Greasy Sousaphone
"Ode on a Grecian Urn" by John Keats (1795-1821)

Thou still unpolished horn ne'er outperformed,
Thou man-child of deep and luscious tone,
Crusty musician, who canst thus transform
A melodic line more smoothly than polished stone:
What once-heard sound haunts about thy bell
Of novices or masters, or of both,
In concert halls or fields of play?
What resonances are these? What composer's quoth?
Of Holst? Vaughn Williams?
Of Donner and Blitzen?

Ah, happy, happy valves! that cannot move
Their frame, nor ever rise from halfway down;
And, happy sousa case, duct-taped,
Forever holding its corpse of renown;
More nasty blats! more nasty, nasty blats!
Forever dented with mouthpiece crammed,
Forever struggling, and forever young;
All breathing serpent that doth enwrap,
That leaves a shoulder disjointed and jammed,
An aching back, and an empty lung.

O Musty smell! O sousaphone! with bore
Of fiberglass or golden brass overwrought,
With gaping holes and depressing dings;
Thou, silent horn, dost tease us out of thought
As doth Sousa: Cold Raincatcher!
When newer models appear pristine and chaste,
Thou shalt remain, in the midst of a younger pro than
Thou, a friend to man, to whom thou say'st,
"Sousas rule. Others drool," — that is all
Ye know in band, and all ye need to know.

Charge of the Blue Bulldogs
"Charge of the Light Brigade" by Alfred Lord Tennyson (1809-1892)

     This adaptation is dedicated to the 1991 Greenwood High School Band who were under the direction of Steve Kesner. In the fall of 1991, they performed Elvis's "American Trilogy" at halftime of a homecoming football game with the local chamber of commerce providing fireworks that were to be set off as the piece concluded. As the band did a backfield move towards the fireworks display, there was a tremendous explosion when all the fireworks accidentally went off at the same time. With amateur firework technicians scattering, a thick cloud of smoke settled over the field so that not only could the band not hear, they could not see either. But the band bravely marched on and as the last fiery burst faded, they emerged from the smoke playing "The Battle Hymn of the Republic." The audience, thinking this perfectly-timed escape from smoke inhalation was planned, gave the band a standing ovation.

Sideline, first hash,
Second hash, onward,
All on the field of fire
Marched the one hundred.
"Forward, the Blue Bulldogs!
March through the smoke!" the drum major said:
Onto the field of fire
Marched the one hundred.

"Forward, the Blue Bulldogs!"
Was there a man dismayed?
Although the marcher knew
Someone had blundered.
Their's not to make reply,
Their's not to reason why,
Their's but to do and fry:
Onto the field of fire
Marched the one hundred.

Roman candles to the right of them,
Firecrackers to the left of them,
Bottle rockets in front of them
Volleyed and thundered;
Pyrotechnics with powerful flare,
Boldly they marched into the glare,

Into the jaws of Death,
Into throes of despair
Marched the one hundred.

Flashed all their brasses bare,
Flashed the woodwinds and the snare,
Twirling the blazing flags in air,
Tossing the batons, while
All the parents wondered.
Plunged in the rising flame
Right through the billows they came;
Cheerleaders and drill teams
Reeled from the flying embers
Coughing and wheezing,
They did retreat, but not,
Not the one hundred.

When can their glory fade?
O the wild charge they made!
All the crowd wondered
Remember the charge they made!
Honor the Blue Bulldogs,
Noble one hundred!

I Heard a Metronome Tick—When I Rushed

"I Heard a Fly Buzz—When I Died" by Emily Dickinson (1830-1886)

I heard a Metronome tick—when I rushed—
The March on the Concert Stage
Was like the Winds of a Storm—
Between the Snow and Ice—

The Tempo varied—had taken its course—
And Pencils were writing fast
For that last Onslaught—when the Judges
Be witnessed—in the Concert Hall—

I wielded my Baton—Conducted away
What tempo of fate be
Performable—and then it was
There interposed a Metronome.

The Trio—uncertain slowing tics—
Between the band— and me—
And then the Pulse hastened—and then
I could not feel the beat—

Here's a cute little ditty I just had to include.

Mary had a little lamb
That learned to play the drum.
And everywhere that Mary went,
She marched to rum-tum-tum.

And now, a few original limericks:

There once was a grouch from Las Vegas
Who performed on the grandest of basses.
From a bow of great length that required great strength
Came tones with the longest of faces.

There once was a vain virtuoso
Who entered the stage maestoso.
But when the solo he muffed, he felt rather rebuffed,
And left the stage piu mosso.

There once was an entrepreneur
Who lost thousands selling manure.
But the man hit it rich when he found a niche—
Getting bands to sell it for tour.

There once was a former cartoonist
Who became an accomplished bassoonist.
When a note was miskeyed, he blamed the poor reed—
He was also a fine opportunist.

There once was an oboe performer
Whose head cold had just overcome 'er.
She wheezed and she sneezed, but the director was pleased—
For 'twas the best tone he'd ever heard from 'er.

There once was a man from Helsinki,
Who played the harp with his pinky.
Till his finger got stuck as the strings he did pluck
And the harp fell and rolled like a Slinky.

There once was a tubist named Stidum
Who always had problems with rhythm.
He'd learn music by rote and ne'er miss a note,
But the rhythm would just not stay with 'im.

There once was a marcher named Pete
Born with two disagreeable feet.
They would haphazardly pound a hole in the ground
When they couldn't agree on the beat.

Bladder Trouble

In my last book, I mentioned ways to avoid lawsuits. This chapter concerns a lawsuit I did not anticipate. I don't think I could have dreamed this one up.

A teen magazine by the name of *Twist* reported a few years ago that a high school freshman sued his band director for not stopping the bus when he needed to use the bathroom. The boy, who wet his pants, says that he got physically sick from the teasing he received from other students after the incident.

Now I have heard everything. A director's whole career potentially goes down the drain (or should I say toilet) because he failed to correctly judge the capacity of a kid's bladder. What really surprises me about the whole thing was that it was a *boy* who sued. He should be ashamed. Real men are supposed to have bladders of steel, bladders capable of great feats of endurance that continue an American masculine tradition dating back to the male pioneers of the Old West who went from the east to the west coast without having to detour once.

Boys aren't as tough as they used to be. I had a male student a few years ago who must have had a bladder the size of a nickel and a very low threshold of pain. On my checklist during his years in band, I added a note to remind him to go to the bathroom before we left on each trip. This still did not prevent an extra stop on some of our longer journeys just for him. And when we stopped, sympathy pains descended upon the rest of the band (including yours truly) like a torrential rain, and what was supposed to be a five minute stop turned into a sixty-minute hiatus. Compounding the problem was the fact that rural gas stations in Arkansas are more suitable for a five-piece country band, not a large marching band. (Our part of Arkansas is mainly a farming region with fields and little tree cover, so "improvising" is not an option.)

I must admit that my lack of sympathy has to do with my maleness. The need to conquer, to arrive, and to accomplish that I inflict on my family during vacations is hard at work on band trips. It's harder for men to pull over for rest room stops because it is a test of our manhood and machismo to see how far we can go before stopping. I remember being on a church trip once, dying of abdominal pains, but I was not going to request a bathroom stop before a woman did. Call it pride if you will; I call it genetics.

Even with a healthy sense of sympathy, it is hard to judge an individual kid's threshold of pain. Not surprisingly, none of my university studies included lessons on band trips and bladder sizes. Usually by the time kids are seniors, I have a fairly accurate estimate of their endurance, but freshmen always throw a kink in the works for which there is no easy solution this side of distributing Depends (bearing the school colors and logo) before each band trip.

It will be interesting to see what the future holds. With the American penchant for legislating everything, there may soon be a federally-mandated requirement that buses stop every thirty minutes for bathroom breaks so that we meet the needs of the bladder-impaired, our newest minority group. Of course, at my age, that may not be so bad.

To the Rear

Completely focused, I swung the pockmarked paddle downward at the intended target. To my horror and shame I missed, striking the student in the back of the legs. And I kept swinging, not out of cruelty but because I felt like I had to hit the right spot. After three or four more unsuccessful attempts, I awoke in a cold sweat, relieved to find myself still in bed.

Corporal punishment has been a subject of controversy for many years. It wasn't until I attended education classes in college that I discovered this. Until then, I thought corporal punishment was a fact of life, having been the recipient of such an approach during my formative years.

My parents had no problem with corporal punishment. I, on the other hand, was firmly opposed to it. Although spanking was a last resort, used only when reasoning and less drastic forms of correction did not work, my mother could swing a pretty good ruler (and later a yardstick as my dimensions widened). There was a short period when she used a wooden paddle that was shaped in the form of a hand. On its surface, in artsy lettering, were painted the words "Mother's Helping Hand" (one of the more unusual craft show items I've ever seen). My father preferred the manual method ("Father's Helping Hand," I guess you could call it).

The first time I received a paddling at school was, ironically, from my junior high band director. Or, more correctly, a thickly muscled coach performed the deed at the behest of our less thickly muscled female director in a kind of tag-team match like one would see in professional wrestling, only this wasn't fake. I was in the seventh grade. My director was giving individual chair tests. I'm not sure why, but she was giving them in the home economics building rather than the bandroom. Before I arrived (I was running late from making up a science test), she gave instructions to my friends in the trumpet section not to play while she returned to the bandroom to get something. When I walked into the room, my colleagues were belting out grotesque noises that threatened to break old windows and young eardrums. I sat down with a friend and actually played some of our music. (Normally I wasn't such a saint, it just so happened I wasn't in a violent mood.) Our director returned and was furious to find a cacophony of sounds like one might find in a cross between New York City traffic and a herd of angry elephants. A silence almost as deafening as the noise we were producing quickly followed her entrance. We were promptly marched to the coach's room, lined up, and whupped.

The only other time I received a paddling at school was later that year (there's just something about seventh grade). It was the last day of school, and I received a paddling in social studies class for verbally counting sheep ("One little sheepie, two little sheepie, etc.") while I had my head down on my desk during an impromptu, teacher-instituted quiet time. Fortunately, my social studies teacher gave a light paddling that was more good-natured than not. It showed some appreciation for my offbeat, if not corny, sense of humor.

I avoided paddlings after seventh grade (no small accomplishment), so the issue was not of real importance to me until my first year of teaching. Since the school district I was entering allowed corporal punishment, I had to decide if it would be a part of my discipline plan.

I decided to use corporal punishment as a last resort and to only give a paddling after a specific warning to the student that if his inappropriate behavior occurred again he would receive one or two "licks." During my first six years, the kids who got into the most trouble with me were my fine arts class students drawn from the general population. One nine-week grading period, I had a class that probably received more paddlings than other classes in all my years combined. I was surprised that I did not contract tendonitis in my right shoulder. I only paddled one band student during my first six years of teaching. By my seventh year, I just decided not to use paddlings anymore. It seemed to me that my last resort was not a last resort after all because I was not involving parents in the process.

Corporal punishment has not left me with any permanent scars (if you don't count a slight shoulder twitch); nor do I believe, when used judiciously, it would do irreparable harm to a student. I would be the last one to judge teachers who choose it as part of their discipline plan, but I just don't see it as necessary. I have found other alternatives that will work. Besides, I sleep a little better at night.

* See Appendix B for some basic discipline tips.

Real World University

After entering the real world of band directing, many directors realize how little their universities prepared them for the experience. Realistically, no school can truly prepare its students for everything. There are some things you just have to *do* to fully understand. I humbly suggest some course offerings that could improve our music schools. Here's the college catalog for what I would call Real World University.

Introduction to Organizational Abbreviations. Learn the meaning of music organization abbreviations, e.g., ASBDA, NBA, MENC, ABA, FBA, ASBOA, NAPBIRT, CBDNA, MTNA, DCI, AGEHR, IAJE, MDA, MPA, NABIM, NAMM, PAS, etc.

Parent Relations 101. Learn how to relate to parents of all types: irate, talkative, irrational, apathetic, overprotective, etc. Discuss potentially controversial issues like chair tests, practice and performance attendance, and classroom behavior.

Marriage Counseling 101. Course designed for prospective spouses of band directors. Preventive in nature. Warns of impending changes in band director spouse that include the contraction of stomach ulcers, migraines, hearing loss, and general dementia.

Speech 101. Introduction to basic band director speeches that can inspire students to greater heights in the musical world. Topics include behavior on buses, PDA (public display of affection), instrument care, school pride, practicing, being kind to gerbils, etc.

Speech 201. Continuation of Speech 101. Includes advanced techniques of throwing batons, knocking over music stands, and simulating heart attacks and strokes.

Fundraising 101. Examines pros and cons of selling various items, e.g., candy, calendars, fruit, toothbrushes, diet plans, toilet lids, deodorant, automobile air fresheners shaped like Gustav Holst, etc.

Advanced Fundraising 201. Examines methods of wrenching money from kids and parents who have owed money for months (hiring repo men, hand-to-hand combat, etc.).

Techniques of Lawsuit Avoidance 101. Survey of how to lawsuit-proof any music program.
Note: This class cannot cover every possible scenario and Real World University claims no responsibility for future cases that may occur that were not covered in class.

Introduction to Cheerleading. An examination of stands tunes and percussion cadences that cheerleaders like best. Introduction of ways to drive cheerleaders crazy like playing the fight song too fast, etc.

Survey of Excuses for Unacceptable Performances. Advanced preparation for future directors looking to keep up with more experienced colleagues. Excuses cover marching and concert band seasons. Note from instructor: This class may not be very interesting because I have only taught it once before.

Sensitivity Training 101. Survey of new musical terms guaranteed not to offend. Examples: digitally challenged (poor technique), acoustically dispossessed (poor balance), and motivationally deficient (lazy).

Special Problems in Marching Band. Group therapy sessions on how to deal with kids who not only march out of step, but out of phase. Limited to forty class members.

Old War Stories 101. Learn how to one-up other band directors by studying the worst band disasters in history.

Band Economics 101. Learn how to use duct tape for every need of your band program from repairing instruments to disciplining students. Required text: *Band on 5 Dollars a Month.*

Beginning Coach Relations 101. Learn the basic techniques of communication with coaches, e.g., grunting, head-butting, slapping rear ends.

Intermediate Coach Relations 201. Survey of stands music most loved by coaches. Study tunes that stir up the competitive fire of their young charges. Also learn what songs to avoid—Sousa marches, love ballads, anything you haven't heard on the radio or TV, and the like.

Advanced Administrator Relations 301. Learn how to deal with coaches once they become administrators. Develop strategies that will help you avoid performing at all football, basketball, soccer, track, golf, cricket, lacrosse, chess, and tiddlywinks competitions.

Repair Basics 101. One-day course. Learn how to oil valves, grease slides, use a spray bottle, and put springs back in place. Also learn how to dial phone number of nearest repair technician to fix all other problems.

Rehearsal Preparations 101. Participants will be required to direct a select group of thirty beginners with attention deficit disorder and extensive juvenile criminal records.

Convention Etiquette 101. Participants will learn how to sneak out of boring clinics unnoticed and sample convention booth fundraiser foods without having to hear a fundraising spiel.

Convention Etiquette 201. Learn how to thwart the efforts of colleagues who unnecessarily extend meetings by asking dumb questions and bringing up controversial topics that will never be resolved and are rehashed at every meeting.

Fundamentals of Junior and Senior Band Director Relations.
Junior high directors learn why senior high band directors think they know it all, and senior high directors learn why junior high directors think they can do it all better.

Psychology of Double Reed Players. Extensive study of double reed players and their love/hate relationship with reeds. Learn how to deal sensitively with them on a "bad reed" day (or week, or month, or longer).

Principles of Lunch Duty. Learning techniques of self-defense that can be used to survive this perilous responsibility. Two such techniques studied in-depth:

using a lunch tray as a shielding device and hurling a burrito with deadly force and accuracy. Note: Students must provide their own burritos.

NOTE: Real World University reserves the right to add courses at a moment's notice and catch one totally off guard.

The Band Director Game

DIRECTIONS:
1. GRADUATE FROM COLLEGE
2. GET A JOB
3. ROLL DICE

(DICE NOT INCLUDED—GET THEM FROM YOUR DRUMMERS)

PRINCIPAL'S FAVORITE SONG IS "LOUIE, LOUIE." GO BACK 2

PRINCIPAL'S FAVORITE WORK IS HOLST'S MILITARY SUITE IN Eb. ADVANCE 1

3 ADVANCED PLACEMENT COURSES SCHEDULED OPPOSITE BAND. GO BACK 1

YOU'RE ASSIGNED 3 STUDY HALLS. GO BACK 2

FOOTBALL TEAM PLAYS 4 PLAY-OFF GAMES. GO BACK 3

BAND RAISES $10,000 SELLING LIGHTBULBS. ADVANCE 2

BAWLED OUT BY MAJORETTE MOTHER. GO BACK 5

ROLL

WOODSTOCK

ALL-STATE TUBA PLAYER MOVES IN. ADVANCE 2

SAX PLAYER MOVES OUT.

LOSE $1,000 SELLING TOOTH-BRUSHES. GO BACK 2

ADVANCE 1

FERMATA LAND — STAY UNTIL ROLLING AN 8 OR ABOVE

The Band Director Game

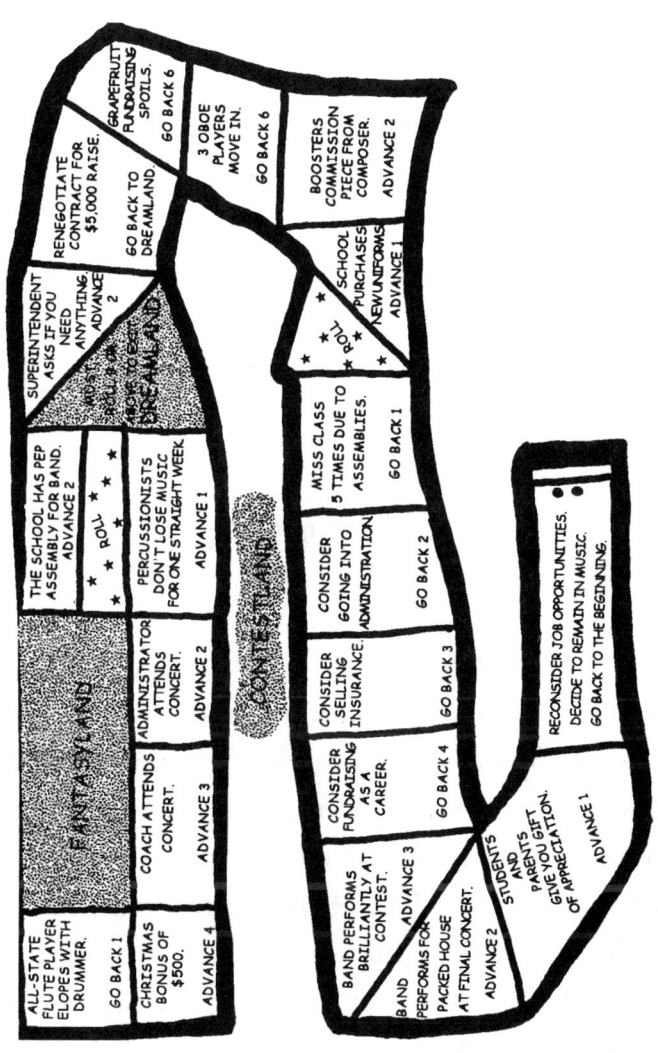

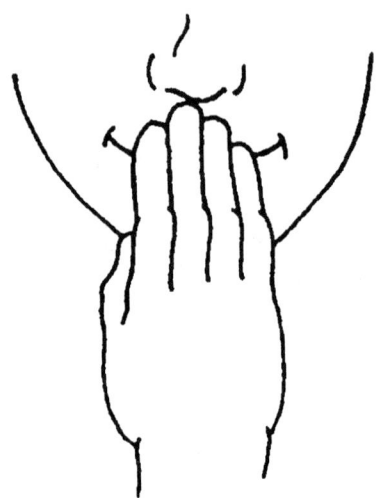

It Goes Without Saying

I like to talk—just ask my former teachers. In elementary school it was not unusual for me to receive grades of B and C in conduct. I wasn't really a troublemaker or disrespectful, I just enjoyed the social scene a little too much and liked to make people laugh, a talent my teachers did not always appreciate.

When I finally did receive that first A in conduct in sixth grade, the feeling was so intoxicating that by ninth grade I earned *almost* straight A's in conduct every grading period. I say almost because I usually had a major lapse in each class. In band I got a C one nine weeks for an incident where I jazzed up my four tune-up notes (G-A-B-C) after a wager with my trumpet buddies. I never did collect on that $1.50 bet. However, I *was* acting better after I learned how to channel my urges into acceptable behavior. I would raise my hand before making what I thought might be a humorous comment. I even made sure the comment had something to do with what was being discussed in class.

I never did reach the goal of straight A's in conduct but only because the high school I attended did not have conduct grades. I admit this was no real disappointment for me because it meant I was free at last!

This lifelong enjoyment of talking presents a challenge when it comes to band rehearsals. Rehearsals are hardly efficient when students have to listen to a director talk more than they play their instruments. I know from experience how frustrating it can be to sit in a band and raise my instrument to play only to have the director continue his discourse on some subject that fascinates him immensely. My college conducting course taught the importance of running efficient rehearsals as well as the time-wasting and demoralizing effects of excessive words.

However, the full import of this never hit home until the day I lost my voice after struggling with a sore throat for two days. My throat red and scratchy, I slowly ate breakfast as I contemplated staying home— what good could I do without being able to speak above a small whisper? But then I reminded myself that there were over 150,000 nonverbal gestures at my disposal (I read that somewhere, maybe *The Bathroom Reader*), so I reasoned that I could summon up enough gestures to survive eight hours of charades.

The day started with a beginning band rehearsal. At first my repertoire of gestures seemed limited to nodding yes or no, but as I warmed up, my arsenal began to grow. Naturally, students took great pleasure in my distress, but they also enjoyed the charades. Not content with just holding up exercise numbers from their method book, I decided to liven things up a bit by acting out such titles as "Lightly Row," "William Tell," "Camptown Races," and "When the Saints Go Marchin' In." Although this wasn't as efficient as simply holding up numbers with my fingers, students became dramatically more enthusiastic as the fun increased.

The high school band also enjoyed the charades, but communication proved to be more difficult than beginning band since the band was not playing from a method book. As the rehearsal progressed, I began to focus more on communicating through conducting gestures. Every musical problem was subject to my baton. Improper dynamics? I would stop the band and silently conduct it the way I wanted it played. Incorrect style or dragging tempo? I would force them to watch the baton. After several stops, the band's concentration level shot sky-high. This heightened concentration was still evident in private lessons later that day. Since I could barely speak, students had to watch and listen very intently. After a while some students even started to whisper comments back to me.

As I reflect back on that day, I realize it was more productive than days my throat was normal. This illness forced me to talk less and be more energetic, animated, and creative on the podium. Could it be that *all* my rehearsals might benefit from more energy and less talking? That probably goes without saying.

Selections from My Private Journal

The following are excerpts from the private journal I plan to publish posthumously or after my death, whichever comes first.

Summer practices are going full tilt. Very busy right now. I forgot the name of my youngest child today. Sent him next door thinking he was the neighbor's kid.

Idea for marching band article: Quick cures for ingrown toenails. Call Dr. Shedd for ideas. Has reached epidemic stage in tuba section.

My principal came into the bandroom today. I thought he was lost. I fainted when he said he just wanted to listen to the band. Revived an hour later in the nurse's office.

Torrential rain at homecoming game. Drummer fell into ditch and never seen again. Good news: we did recover bass drum mallets.

Contest show idea for next year: salute to Paul Anka. Close with his 1972 hit "You're Havin' My Baby." Have flag line dress as if pregnant.

Got back from away football game at 11:30 p.m. Last parent arrived at 1:30 a.m. Raise funds next year for a transporter room.

The football players sent me a petition requesting more songs that will fire them up. Remember to pull out "Chariots of Fire," "You Light up My Life," "Brian's Song," and "Under the Sea" for the next ballgame.

It is the day before our biggest marching contest. I am confused. Cannot decide whether I am homicidal or suicidal.

Made a big mistake today by making an offhanded remark about the excessive weight of our majorettes. Should be receiving call from parent at any minute. Selling insurance looks great right now. Maybe I should *buy* some more.

I must begin diet as soon as candy fundraiser is over. Could barely zip up pants today.

Whoever said, "There is no such thing as a dumb question," was wrong.

Research: Are there any Barbies that come with a band instrument? Is Barbie too good to be in band?

Little trolls are striking again. They are sneaking into the bandroom and dropping empty plastic bottles and other trash onto the floor. It could not possibly be my students (or so they say).

Thought: If someone owned a solid, nice-looking, but slightly dusty hurdy-gurdy, would it be called a sturdy-purdy-durdy-hurdy-gurdy?

Concert band contest is tomorrow. I must get some sleep tonight. The last five nights I have dreamed that I am conducting *First Suite in Eb* with a pickled herring.

Are there any seventh graders in heaven? Do they play instruments? If so, I am not sure I can take it.

Nobody understands me. Sometimes I think I must be speaking another language. "No man is an island"? I am at the most a peninsula.

I lost it in beginning band class today. I ran from the room screaming, "All notes are *not* created equal!" over and over again. I must remain composed tomorrow.

Composition idea: a salute to woodchucks. Have a B section where performers jut out top teeth and make rhythmic sounds with teeth against wet bottom lip.

Coda:

Practical Suggestions for Directors

Open Letter to Piano Teachers

If being a piano teacher is anything like being a band director, it must seem thankless at times. You teach students for years, tirelessly encouraging them to make the most of their talent, only to have them quit when a new interest catches their eye. When kids quit band, I get discouraged looking back at what seems like wasted time, but I believe their exposure to music, however brief, will make them better than if they had not studied at all. I suppose piano teachers go through some of the same emotions when losing a student, particularly a talented one, but perhaps I can soften the blow by testifying that students who have had even as little as a year of piano are a tremendous benefit to band programs.

Students who have had piano lessons gain an important introduction to performing music. I have had little problem recruiting former and current piano students into my band program because of the background they received from piano teachers. Students with piano experience know the note names for both treble and bass clefs and progress more rapidly on a new instrument.

French horns have inherent acoustical difficulties, and if beginning players have some piano experience, they can locate the correct pitches on the keyboard when practicing at home. Each year I select students who have had piano lessons to be percussionists because they quickly grasp the concepts of playing bells, xylophone, marimba, and timpani. When I need brass and woodwind players to fill out percussion ensembles, I choose those with keyboard backgrounds.

Piano students who continue studies are particularly valuable to band programs as accompanists for solo and ensemble events. In musicals, pianists serve as rehearsal accompanists and sometimes cover string parts on a synthesizer. Accomplished pianists are essential to jazz programs.

Whether students take piano lessons one year or ten, they prove invaluable to band directors, who realize how much they owe you, the piano teacher. So for band directors everywhere, I just want to say, "thank you."

Student Conductors

During marching season, directors generally make good use of student leadership with color guard captains, squad leaders, section leaders, and drum majors. However, when concert season begins, many of these positions naturally dissolve and student responsibility diminishes. One way to maintain a greater degree of student leadership is through the use of a student conductor.

There are several advantages to having a student conductor. First, it gives at least one student an opportunity to gain invaluable experience working with a band in a concert setting and a positive experience may make him or her consider pursuing a music degree in college. A student conductor can also direct the band when the director is absent (but a substitute should be present to help monitor the band's behavior). Finally, having a student conductor gives the band director a chance to teach conducting skills at the high school level. Ironically, this can motivate the band director to evaluate his own techniques of conducting and make necessary adjustments.

Hold auditions for the position of student conductor as soon as possible after marching season. You will need to decide if drum majors are eligible. One advantage of making them ineligible is that it gives another student an opportunity to front the band. Have a meeting of all potential candidates and explain exactly what tryout procedures will be followed. Distributing a copy of the judge's score sheet to each student would be very helpful. Schedule required practice sessions (apart from the band) that candidates must attend if they are to audition. This ensures that those trying out are serious about the position and will do a respectful job in front of the band. Practice sessions should cover all aspects of the audition and a mock tryout would be helpful. Reserve suggestions of improvements to practice sessions to avoid embarrassing potential student conductors in front of the band.

Several elements should make up the tryout. Students should be able to demonstrate beat patterns for several time signatures (2/4, 3/4, 4/4, 5/4, slow 6/8) in various styles (legato, marcato, and staccato) and tempos. Another aspect of the tryout should be the direction of a chorale. An easy, short chorale enables inexperienced conductors to concentrate on the fundamentals of conducting and helps build confidence. The students should be able to demonstrate a clear preparatory beat, vary the dynamics through the use of the left hand, vary the tempo, and give clear releases.

Potential student directors should also direct a fairly short concert selection. It is important that a work be short so that the tryout can be finished during one rehearsal. The endurance of the band must also be considered. You may decide to let students select their own pieces, but standardizing the tryout makes judging easier. It is important that the work selected require different conducting styles and beat patterns. Students should be judged on the same factors as the chorale with additional emphasis on setting appropriate tempos, giving clear cues, providing good eye contact, and displaying a thorough knowledge of the score.

If possible, the scoring system should take into account how much each potential candidate has contributed to the band program that particular year. If your band program uses a merit system, taking a small percentage of the candidates' merit total and adding it to their other scores is effective. This gives a slight, but deserved, advantage to students who have been strong leaders throughout the year.

Bring in two or three directors whom you respect for their conducting skills to judge. You may or may not be one of the judges yourself, depending on your own philosophy. Student conductor candidates should draw numbers to determine the order of appearance. Emphasize to the band members the importance of maintaining as much concentration the last time the selections are played as the first time. This helps ensure a fair tryout for each candidate.

Once a candidate is chosen, be sure to give that person some publicity through releases in the school announcements, the school newspaper, and a local newspaper.

The next task is to help the student conductor find a suitable piece of music to conduct at a concert. Help him select a work which is well within his ability to conduct and the band's ability to perform. The music should be at a level which the young conductor can concentrate on the nuances of conducting—not just beating out difficult passages every day and trying to hold the ensemble together.

Personally work with the student conductor on a weekly basis. Let him be a regular part of the warm up routine so he can become more comfortable working with his peers. Supply the student with reading materials that will help to improve his knowledge of conducting.

Before a performance, make sure that the student knows what is expected in terms of concert attire and how to acknowledge the applause properly so he doesn't make an awkward exit from the stage. You may choose to present him with a certificate or plaque after he conducts.

Creating the position of student conductor provides an invaluable opportunity for some music students and is a special way of passing on this important skill and art we call conducting. Make it an important position, and you will soon have a new and valuable tradition as a part of your band program.

Convention Fatigue

There's nothing quite like the fatigue that overtakes you at a band convention. It sneaks up in the middle of convention concerts, and its full-blown effect hits once you return home. I often wonder why I feel so tired at the end of the convention because it doesn't seem as though I really did anything all that strenuous. Perhaps it is the cumulative effect of traveling, staying on my feet all day, late-night chats over hot chocolate or coffee, attending clinics on how to control the percussion section, band association breakfasts at 4:00 a.m., and lugging bags of free demo tapes and other convention freebies.

You might wonder what convention fatigue has to do with programming, but I see fatigue as something that is being ignored when directors plan their programs for conventions. At the Midwest convention, some of the senior bands have to perform for ninety minutes, and even under the best of circumstances it is difficult to capture an audience's attention for that long. The challenge escalates when the audience suffers from advanced stages of convention fatigue. It is essential to keep the program engaging because with poorly paced programs the ears have a tendency to rebel and resist incoming information, kind of like what would happen if you listened to about thirty Bach fugues and twenty Sousa marches in a row.

I do feel a bit guilty nitpicking what are otherwise fantastic performances produced by exceptional young musicians and their directors. Although comments I hear about Midwest performances are overwhelmingly positive, when there is a negative comment it generally goes like this—"Great band. Boring program." Observing audience responses confirms this observation. It seems a shame to work so hard and then bore an audience with a poorly paced program. Don't get me wrong—the music selected is usually topnotch. It's just that it might not need to be placed in that particular program. Most bands seem to err by playing too many slow to medium-paced selections or twentieth-century works that are hard to listen to for extended periods. A more upbeat program is needed for long concerts.

Although Midwest has stipulations that limit programming possibilities somewhat, it is still possible to provide a program with enough diversity to combat the onset of convention fatigue. For example, in 1997 the Lake Braddock Symphonic Band from Burke, Virginia (Ray Holder, conductor), performed a varied program with great musicality and skill. It wasn't just the group's outstanding playing that made the performance great; it was the fact that it was applied to diverse and interesting music. The band's program ran as follows (my comments in parenthesis):

"Allegro Vivace" from Jerry Bilik's *Symphony for Band*. (Upbeat start.)

Elsa's Procession to the Cathedral arranged by Bourgeois. (Antiphonal trumpets add to an already dramatic ending.)

Eagle Pride March by Mark Seaman. (Grade 1 Quick-Step.)

Slidefest arranged by Michael Davis. (Upbeat change of pace featuring trombone section.)

For Unto Us by Handel/Curnow. (Medium tempo Grade 2 excerpt from Handel's *Messiah*.)

"Ritmico" from Dance Movements by Philip Sparke. (Latin American feel.)

Swan Lake Suite Mvt. II by Tschaikovsky/Lake (Slow and beautiful music.)

Manhattan Beach March by Sousa. (Nice contrast to previous selection.)

Wedding Dance by Press/Johnston/Fennell. (Up-tempo, really keeps the program moving in the latter stages of the performance.)

Concerto for Tuba, Mvt. III (Rondo) by James Barnes. (Nice solo feature.)

1812 Overture by Tchaikovsky/Hindsley. (Bass drums placed strategically around the performance hall made for a dramatic, though startling, ending!)

Contrast that program with the one that follows, which would probably be performed late in the evening for an audience that had just eaten a lavish meal at a Chicago restaurant.

Fanfare or March (Good start.)

ABA Type Grade 3 (Things are still okay.)

Slow Grade 2 Selection (Convention fatigue begins its assault.)

Three or four movements of a work using modern compositional techniques (Occasional accented dissonant chord awakes you from deep sleep; dreams usually resemble science fiction movies.)

Another slow selection (Hit the snooze button; where are the cannons from 1812 Overture when you need them?)

Four-movement Renaissance selection (Potentially interesting in another time and place; smattering of parents' applause brings you back from comatose state.)

Solo Feature (Good idea, well-performed, continued dissonance sends you back to na-na land.)

One More Stab at Refined Serialism (Z-Z-Z-Z-Z-Z; even those immune to convention fatigue are long gone.)

Rousing March (Good finish.)

Even at conventions where the music selection is entirely up to the performing group's discretion, I have seen fine military bands show the same tendency. One convention I attended dedicated every single selection on the program to the same composer—great composer, great music, but too much of a good thing. Yet others show a refreshing ability to lighten up by playing some lighter concert fare—not arrangements of current pop tunes mind you, but some stirring arrangements of classics by famous jazz or Broadway composers.

Convention bands seem influenced by what they perceive as a sophisticated musical audience. Probably the most well-received performer at our Arkansas Bandmasters Association Convention in the last several years was the Mr. Jack Daniel's Original Silver Cornet Band. Needless to say, it wasn't a program dedicated to twelve-tone arrangements of Dixieland tunes! The program was meticulously performed, upbeat, varied, entertaining, and just what a bunch of directors and their spouses needed before heading off to the trials of marching band.

Directors should consider the unique circumstances of a convention audience and program accordingly. Great music organized properly can excite even the most convention-fatigued audiences.

Theory X
or
Theory Y

My dad, a university instructor, has taught business courses for many years. His thoughts on business have had an impact on how I run my band. This is something I wrote many years ago based on some of his business ideas. The ideas are still very relevant, however. My daughter says this chapter sounds too "intelligent." (In other words, not like me!)

Motivation has long been an important topic of study in many fields. Theologians, psychologists, sociologists, scientists, business leaders, and educators alike have delved into the mysteries of motivation, striving to understand why humans behave the way they do. More specifically, music educators are constantly concerned with the "hows" of motivating students to fully enjoy and appreciate the utilitarian and aesthetic aspects of music. Writings in music education have focused on such motivational factors as extrinsic and intrinsic rewards, student and teacher self-concept, teacher personality traits, music selection, and praise. While these studies are important and useful, there is one aspect of motivation that, if overlooked, can undermine the rest.

In *The Human Side of Enterprise,* Douglas McGregor, the late Sloan Professor of Management at MIT, presented a convincing—though untested—argument that most management actions result from whatever view of human behavior managers hold. McGregor proposed that all managers hold certain assumptions about human behavior, either implicit or explicit, that influence their management style. He categorized these assumptions as either Theory X or Theory Y.

FIGURE 1 – Theory X and Theory Y

Theory X	Theory Y
1. The average human being has an inherent dislike of work and is basically lazy.	1. People have an innate tendency to work and to produce.
2. Most people must be coerced, controlled, and threatened to get results.	2. People will exercise self-direction and self-control if given the opportunity.
3. The average person has little ambition and prefers to be directed.	3. The average human being accepts and seeks responsibility.

Theory X assumes that people are innately lazy, dislike work, and will avoid it if at all possible. It also implies that people lack responsibility, have little ambition, and must be coerced, controlled, and threatened to achieve high performance standards.

Theory Y implies that humans can be self-directed and creative if provided with the proper environment to maximize their potential. It also assumes that the average human being looks for additional responsibility and autonomy on the job and does not need to be coerced into doing responsible work.

McGregor believed that assumptions had a large impact on how management-employee relationships were structured. He also saw assumptions as determinants of the kinds of rewards and penalties utilized, the character of the communication process in the organization, and the type of behavior exhibited by managers towards employees and vice versa.

Although McGregor's ideas were concerned with the business community, they have important implications for music educators.

FIGURE 2 – TWO SETS OF ASSUMPTIONS ABOUT STUDENTS
(Adapted from the BNA Film "Theory X and Theory Y, Part I" by Saul Gellermin)

THEORY X	THEORY Y
Students need specific instructions on what to do and how to do it; important decisions are none of their business	Students need ever-increasing understating; they need to grasp the meaning of activities in which they are participating.
Students naturally resist change; they prefer to stay in old ruts.	Students tire of routine and enjoy new experiences.
Students have little concern beyond their immediate, material interest.	Students seek to give meaning to their lives by identifying with others of similar interest and developing a sense of community.
Certain musical requirements are primary and must be done. Students are selected, trained, and fitted to predetermined responsibilities.	Students mainly seek self-realization; responsibilities are designed, adjusted, and fitted to students.
The main factor keeping students productive is their fear of failure, punishment, or ridicule	The main factor keeping students productive is their desire to achieve personal and social goals.
Students' attitudes are formed by heredity, childhood, and youth; as they get older they become static; you cannot teach an old dog new tricks.	Students constantly grow; it is never too late to learn; students enjoy increasing their knowledge capabilities.
Students expect and depend on direction from the music teacher; they do not want to think for themselves.	Students close to the situation realize what is needed and are capable of self-direction.
Students are normally lazy; they hate practicing; they prefer to do nothing.	Students are naturally active; they set goals and enjoy working toward them.
Students will get away with anything they can.	Students are basically responsible and if placed in the proper learning environment will act accordingly.
Students appreciate being treated with courtesy.	Students crave genuine respect from teachers and fellow students.

Implications for Band Directors

An examination of **Figure 2** will reveal various assumptions that all band directors hold to some degree, either implicitly or explicitly.

Those who hold to Theory X tend to be authoritarian and directive, while those who operate under Theory Y recognize their interdependence with students and build the students' notions of self-control, collaboration, and participation in decision making. It is useful to recognize that the average music teacher probably combines traits from both columns.

The significance of McGregor's Theory X and Theory Y lies in the fact that it enables music teachers to identify their own personal assumptions about their students. The identification of personal assumptions is important because they have a tremendous impact on the way things are led, taught, and organized.

Probably the most disturbing aspect of teacher assumptions is that they are reflected in self-fulfilling prophecy. That is, whatever the music educator expects from the students is exactly what he receives. For example, a band director assumes that band students do not like to practice or work hard and that they have to be threatened to get results. These assumptions lead to perceptions of band students as a bunch of lazy goof-offs. These assumptions and perceptions, when combined, cause the director to be more punitive and directive toward his students. This kind of behavior can produce the "I don't care" attitude and behavior he used to validate his initial Theory X assumptions. It is a never-ending cycle.

Another example of how the self-fulfilling prophecy might occur would be in a situation like the following: A director is taking the band on a trip which includes an overnight stay at a hotel. The director, a diehard X-type, says to the group before its departure, "I know you kids are going to try to get away with a lot of mischief on this trip, but don't you try anything because if I catch you the consequences will be severe. You just try to slip a fast one on me!" After a statement like that, there will probably be some to accept the challenge. The point is not that it is wrong to follow Theory X (neither Theory X nor Theory Y is inherently good or bad), but the director should not let his assumptions affect his situation negatively. He could just as easily say, "We are going on an important trip tomorrow, and I know you will want to act responsibly and represent your band, school, and community in an exemplary way. However, because some students in the past have made some mistakes, I would like to explain the consequences of certain types of inappropriate behavior." This will not eliminate all potential problems, but it is a good start.

Three final points need to be made about Theory X and Theory Y. First, Theory Y can also be carried to an extreme. Using the previous example, one can see that a band director holding too strongly to Theory Y might put so much confidence in the students' responsible nature that guidelines for proper behavior are not outlined and anarchy might result.

Second, it is important not to confuse Theory X and Theory Y with personality traits. Theory X teachers are not necessarily mean and Theory Y teachers nice. A music teacher who follows Theory X can be as cheerful and good-natured but still run a basically autocratic organization.

Finally, it is important to remember that neither theory is necessarily good or bad. Both are merely sets of assumptions which educators have about human nature and, more specifically, their students. Although few will adhere to either theory in every particular, there would seem to be a central pattern in each individual's social behavior, a pattern derived from a complicated host of past experiences. Music educators should realize that the structure of our music programs and the equality of teacher-student relationships are reflected in (and are reflections of) the assumptions we hold about the people with whom we work. Understanding our assumptions will be a positive step toward motivating students to develop musically rewarding lives.

Likes and Suggestions

Directors are constantly looking for ways to improve their programs. They consult with respected colleagues, read professional journals, attend clinics, take graduate classes, and often simply rely on their own ingenuity. But in their search, many overlook a gold mine of information—their own students.

Simply handing students sheets of paper and asking them to list what they like about your program and how it might be improved can be tremendously helpful. Although this is a fairly easy approach, there are some important guidelines to follow.

Feedback should be solicited on a periodic basis. Twice a year is ideal for band programs—once after marching season and again after concert season.

The submission of feedback should be on an anonymous basis. This ensures that what the students tell you is open and honest. It also increases the possibility of personal attacks on you, but helpful comments that might be suppressed if the students have to identify themselves will more than make up for a few personal insults.

List various aspects of the program on a blackboard. Listing elements such as jazz band, solo and ensemble, concerts, rehearsals, music performed, private lessons, etc., will stimulate the group's thinking and provide for a wider range of suggestions. You may even ask specific questions about their preference on particular issues.

Ask the students what they like. This is a positive way to solicit feedback. It can serve as a source of encouragement to you and also aid you in determining what aspects of your program should be maintained. Asking the students what they like also serves to balance the negative comments you may receive about some aspect of your program. For example, if ten students dislike the summer practice schedule, but ten prefer it, you will need to consider both sides before making any adjustments.

Request suggestions for improvement. Stress to the students that you do not want petty gripes, but *concrete* ways to improve things.

To gain maximum benefit from this plan, follow these guidelines when examining the results.

List comments. Write down each comment made; when a like or suggestion recurs, put a tick mark by the comment. It is important to total similar comments because this indicates which issues your students feel more strongly about. However, singular comments are still important and may have the potential to influence the entire group.

Compare totals. Look at the ratio of likes to suggestions. If there is one like to every three suggestions, work toward improving your program to the point where there are three likes to every one suggestion. It is important at this point not to be defensive but reflective. Be willing to take a hard, honest look at your program and understand where the students are coming from.

Respond as soon as possible. Students should see some results of their suggestions or they will quickly perceive that you found their ideas of no value. Obtaining feedback in the future will be more difficult if they never saw any results the first time.

When discussing the students' responses, mention the "likes" first. This gets things started in a positive way and provides a chance to talk about all the good things in the program.

When responding to the students' suggestions, avoid becoming defensive. To stand up before the group, read every suggestion and explain why it is unfair, untrue, or impossible to implement will do nothing but discourage the students. On a controversial policy or practice that you think should not change, explain the whys behind the particular policy or practice. Students are more likely to respond positively when they understand the reasons behind certain procedures, but make sure your reasons are justifiable and sound. Also acknowledge the legitimacy of their suggestions and state how you plan to implement improvement.

Use this simple solicitation of likes and suggestions and you will be amazed at the great ideas students provide. It may take more openness and courage on your part to follow this procedure, but students who are volunteering their time and energy deserve to be heard.

Beginning Band Night

Most directors realize the important role that communication plays in running a successful band program. Effective dialogue with administrators, the community, fellow teachers, parents, and students is vital and efforts to inform and receive feedback from others should be a top priority.

Every year a new group enters this web of communication—beginning band members and their parents. When my own children began elementary school, I became frightfully aware of how frustrating it is for parent and child when the child comes home with foggy ideas about an upcoming field trip, a special school project, homework completion dates, money needed for snacks, t-shirts, book fairs, jewelry sales, and so on. These ongoing experiences with my own children have caused me to reevaluate and improve our program's method of working with beginning band students and their parents.

Imagine the inexperienced parents' bewilderment when their child's brand new instrument (or possibly an old one borrowed from their Aunt Flotilla) comes home for the first time. Many questions are bound to arise:

- "Are you sure it's put together that way?"
- "How do you clean this thing?"
- "How should my child practice?"
- "How much should she practice?"
- "Will he always sound like this?"
- "What have we gotten ourselves into?"
- "Can I have my money back?"

To help answer these questions and many others, it is helpful to organize a beginning band night. The following suggestions can help you get your first beginning band night off to a good start. Of course you should tailor these ideas to your own situation.

Two weeks before school begins, send a letter to the parents of all registered beginning band students. Include a welcome and some basic information on what you will be doing the first couple of weeks in band. Include the dates of the rental meeting (if applicable) and the beginning band night. If possible, hold the beginning band night within two days of the rental night. Explain what you want to accomplish at the meeting and outline what will be covered. Suggest that if a parent cannot attend, some adult relative should accompany the child. Sending the letter two weeks before school should eliminate most conflicts. Also send reminder notes once school has started.

When school begins, emphasize daily to beginning band students the importance of the meeting. Tell them that if they are not there, they will miss a lot of information which will help get them off to a fast start. Provide another copy of the mail-out to those who did not receive one for one reason or another. There is no sure way to get all the students and parents to attend, but there are several ways to encourage attendance, and if used singly or in combination, they may prove effective. Several possibilities are telling the class that only those who come to beginning band night will be able to get out their instrument the next day, offering bonus points to those who attend, and telling students who are using school instruments that their parents must come to sign the school check-out form for that instrument and pay necessary maintenance fees (if applicable). Also, if possible, call all beginning band parents and invite them personally.

Schedule the meetings so that a quick, yet thorough coverage of all the instruments is possible. Below is a sample schedule:

        6:00-7:00   Brass
        7:15-8:15   Woodwinds
        8:30-9:30   Percussion

A fifteen-minute cushion is added so that you can answer questions, welcome new arrivals, check out instruments, etc. Lengthen this time if necessary.

Each meeting should follow the same basic agenda. Organize this section carefully, because it's very important that the parents perceive your program as well-organized. The following is a sample agenda.

Welcome. Introduce yourself and other instructors in the program, including educational backgrounds and experiences and any other pertinent personal information. Enthusiastically give a brief rundown of your goals for the program as a whole. Stress the reasons for music study and its importance.

Band booster information. You may want to allow your band booster president to say a few words about the function of the band booster organization and have sign-up sheets for various activities that need parental involvement.

Band policies. Explain discipline policies, grading policies, and other program guidelines. Make sure you have administration approval for all the information you provide.

Performance dates. Hand out a schedule of the year's band events. Emphasize the importance of all performances and concerts. Some parents don't realize the link between performances and the music instruction the students receive each day. To others, missing a concert is no worse than missing a Saturday soccer match. If your band participates in solo and ensemble events, explain what that will entail.

General instrument maintenance. Discuss how to assemble and disassemble the instrument properly. Show students and parents how to apply various oils and greases. Explain what procedures should not be attempted, like extracting stuck mouthpieces with pliers and ruining leadpipes. Reed players and their parents should learn the basics of reed care. Tell parents how instrument repairs are handled and method of payment.

Practice. Tell the parents how much you expect the students to practice. Explain the most effective ways to practice. Suggest items like music stands, metronomes, mutes, boxes of reeds, extra music books, and other items as Christmas and birthday gifts.

Instrument switches. It may help you to warn parents that some instrument switches may be necessary if their child is having problems on a particular instrument.

Curriculum. Explain what teaching materials will be used over the course of the year's study and the following years as well. Parents will be impressed with a comprehensive course of musical study.

Playing basics. Discuss and demonstrate proper posture, breath control, hand positions, and embouchures. Percussionists should learn how to hold the sticks properly and produce even strokes with the proper wrist motion. End the session with students jointly producing sounds on their instruments.

Beginning Band Night

Although it takes another evening out of a very busy week, a well-organized beginning band night can prove to be a catalyst for a very successful year with new students and their parents. You will probably find that many of these parents become involved in many aspects of your program due to the positive impression they gained on beginning band night. Maintain your communication with these parents as their children progress through your program and reap the benefits.

Creative Beginning Band Classes

One challenge faced by directors of beginning bands is to find ways to repeat technical exercises in beginning method books in such a way that students learn them thoroughly yet do not become increasingly bored upon each repetition. Besides the traditional methods of clapping, singing, or counting the rhythms verbally, there are other techniques of repeating exercises which will aid in maintaining a beginning student's interest.

Daily review. Begin each rehearsal by playing exercises which the group has already mastered. This serves as a good warm-up and gets the class started out positively. This also gives students who may be a little behind the others a chance to improve their performance on the exercises reviewed.

Isolation. Isolate troublesome measures and repeat them. Rehearse an exercise beginning with the last measure, gradually working back toward the beginning. Stress to the students the importance of isolating troublesome measures when they are practicing privately.

Bonus points. While advanced players are generally more self-conscious about playing alone in front of the class, beginners are usually very eager to "show their stuff." Use this to your advantage by asking for volunteers to play new exercises for bonus points.

Mouthpiece buzzing. Instead of having the brass players inactive (or getting into trouble) while the woodwinds are playing, ask them to buzz the selected exercise while the woodwinds play.

Airing. When working with one section, have the other members of the class "air" the exercise. (Airing is the process of blowing air into the instrument without producing a tone while practicing the fingerings or positions.)

Subtraction. Begin an exercise with the complete class and subtract one section upon each repetition.

Addition. Add a section upon each repetition.

Student conductors. Teach students the basic conducting patterns and let them conduct some of the exercises while other members of the class play. This adds just enough change to make playing an exercise several times interesting each time.

Watch the director. See how well the students watch by cutting off at unpredictable places in the exercise. With young players it will probably require several attempts before the release is together. The students enjoy the "suspense" involved in this.

Tempo variation. Have all the members of the class stand up and raise their music stands where they can see the music. Then select an exercise, preferably one testing technical skills, and play it several times, slowly the first time and faster with each repetition. Students should sit down on their first mistake. The last remaining player standing should receive bonus points.

Say the note names. Ask different sections to say or sing an exercise using the note names in rhythm while fingering on the instruments. This will help students develop the ability to think note names while playing.

Solo playing. Designate certain measures of a selected exercise to be for a soloist (or a duet) with other members entering at the measure you dictate.

Musical expression. Vary dynamic levels and tempos in an expressive way upon each repetition. Ask students for their ideas on how an exercise might be performed differently, yet tastefully.

Duets and rounds. Many beginning method books contain duets and rounds. Repetition of these kinds of exercises greatly improves the ensemble skills of young players. Divide students into groups of two to six. Select a team name for each group and then let all the groups perform the selected exercise. After the performance, identify the group that performed the piece the best and give suggestions for improvement to all the groups. I call the first group to perform a selection the best two times (only have the groups play it once on any one day) "The Champs." This process sometimes takes several days to complete.

Outplay the director. Challenge students to play an exercise better than you. If they do, give them bonus points. This serves as a strong motivator for the band directors to brush up on *their* secondary instruments!

Test previews. The day before a playing test, ask for volunteers to perform the test alone. After students play the test, tell them what was good, what they need to improve upon, and what their test scores will be if they play it like that the next day. This gives all the students an idea of what standards they must reach.

Add auxiliary percussion. This works particularly well on exercises with a Latin, jazz, or rock feel. All class members enjoy playing with the new sounds added. Let some of the non-percussionists play the added instruments also.

CD and cassette accompaniment. Many class methods now provide background accompaniments for exercises in their respective band books. Students really enjoy these.

Special request review. Periodically select a day (Fridays and days before holidays work well) when students can select the exercise they would like to play. Any exercise which the band has played previously is acceptable. Students often enjoy playing the first few exercises they ever learned—they can hardly believe that those exercises used to be *so hard*.

Preview. At the end of rehearsals introduce a new exercise to stimulate interest in the next day's rehearsal. Tell the students that they can play the exercise for bonus points the next day.

Use these techniques with beginning band students and not only will there be an improvement in fundamentals, but an increased enjoyment of band as well.

Appendix A

On The Selection of Music for the Marching Band

By Dr. Kenneth Raessler

One of the highest compliments I can give a writer is to read something and think, "I wish I had written that!" This is one of those articles. It lists the myriad of musical preferences held by various factions of the community. Band directors would do well to heed these outside influences (at their own peril). Special thanks to Dr. Kenneth R. Raessler for his permission to use and adapt it a little. Dr. Raessler is Professor of Music Emeritus, Texas Christian University.

Superintendent of schools. The taste of this person is usually eclectic, but he likes to hear music he knows. Consequently, his opinions are unpredictable. One thing is certain—the opinions need to be carefully considered.

The director of curriculum. The taste of this person lies midway between country/western and the Romantic era. The key here is "schmaltz."

Appendix A

The director of elementary education would like to hear what could be done with some of the all-time gospel favorites—"The Holy City," "Jesus Loves the Little Children," etc. Since no words would be rendered, there should be no problem with separation of church and state.

The high school principal has no opinion—he avoids hearing the band as much as possible.

The school board president. Absolutely anything which pleases the football ticket holders in rows AA to MM in the reserved seat section. (Music popular in the 50's would work best here.)

The director of public relations has been looking forward for years to a circus theme with all the well-known circus music, balloons, clowns, and horses.

School board members. Each has a vested-interest request just for them: "You'll Never Walk Alone," "Pennsylvania Six Five Thousand," "Star Dust," and "We Are the World."

Football coaching staff. They are open to any music, since they never hear it anyway, as long as the band gets off the field in the allotted time to avoid the team's being penalized. Also, do not play during the game — the team cannot hear the signals.

"The Band Should Play More at Football Games" group. In the interest of the school spirit, they want the band to keep playing pep songs during the football game.

Football team. They do not concern themselves with the band music, but do attempt to contribute to the overall morale of the band by labeling them in endearing ways as Band Buddies, Bandies, etc.

Football parents. All music should inspire team spirit because the raison d'etre for band is to support athletics. Also, the band should cheer more and provide a pep band for the basketball team.

The athletic booster club. This group concerns itself only with athletic matters; however, it does feel that the school district shows partiality to the band parents by allowing them to run the concession stand at football games and take trips to Disney World.

Cheerleaders. The cheerleaders will always cheer for the band at football games regardless of the music selected. They will not attend competitions since it is not in their contract.

The student body. This large group has a strong preference for rock, so they listen to their "boxes" during halftime.

Band parents. The majority of this group never really gets to hear the band because they are selling hot dogs during halftime of the football games to people who would rather support the band financially than listen to them.

Music supervisor. This person just hopes everyone likes the music. He has long since lost his musical taste.

Jazz buffs. They are pleased that a few of the jazz all-time greats are being explored by the marching band, but the director needs to be more discriminating with regard to the quality of most of the jazz chosen.

Classical music buffs. These folks are pleased that the caliber of music played on the field has grown from marches to music of genuine quality, but never hear the band unless they have a child or grandson on the football team.

Symphony orchestra members. This elite group is of the firm opinion that music of the higher order should never be prostituted by being performed on the football field.

Citizens for the Preservation of Patriotism and Alma Maters. They like shows with American flags of all sizes and plenty of patriotic music.

The "They Did Not Play One Song I Knew" club. Every competition lost by the band brings this one to the fore. They are presently compiling a list of the songs they know to assure the band of a winning season.

The general citizenry. They really don't know or care what the band plays because they attend neither football games nor competitions; however, they relay opinions received from friends who do have opinions.

Radio and TV commentators. They do not really care what bands play, just as long as it lasts long enough to cover five commercials.

Band director. His taste is not an issue. He is hired to please others.

Band members. Their opinions do not matter either. They are simply there to entertain.

Appendix B

Basic Discipline Tips

For any potential classroom problem, there should be a reasonable, specific, clearly-stated consequence. Also, have a plan of rewards for correct behaviors. The policies you propose should be approved by your principal. There are few things more professionally embarrassing than being overruled by a principal on a discipline issue.

State the *first* day of class exactly what you expect from your students. I allow students to play before class begins, but once the director steps on the podium all playing and talking ceases. I tell them that it is a waste of time to ask them to be quiet since they know I am ready to rehearse when I step onto the podium. If I step off the podium I allow the kids to talk quietly while I attend to some individual student need. I try to keep the podium maintained as a type of "holy ground," only stepping on it when I mean business. If there is a short break of some kind where a looser atmosphere is warranted, I step down. I begin this procedure (with never an exception) from their beginning year onward. There might be a problem

Appendix B

getting cooperation from older students you "inherit" from another band director, but be *consistent* with the young ones and it will pay off. Have specific consequences for playing at inappropriate times and follow them. The following plan will work:

First offense (warning): Stern warning and statement of consequence if behavior continues.

Second offense: Student must put instrument up and sit in an area where he will no longer disturb the group.

Third offense: Call parents or have the student call the parents with you present.

Fourth offense: Conference with principal and parents.

I allow each kid one warning per class period. It is on the second offense of that class period that the consequences of repeated bad behavior are enacted. If a student has had to put his instrument away (second offense), he will have to call his parents the next time he goes beyond the first warning. The next time he passes the first warning, he will have a conference with the principal and me.

It is also important that you reinforce *positive* behaviors. If a student has been warned for playing his instrument at inappropriate times or something similarly disruptive, catch him acting good (no matter how hard that may be) and say something like, "Mark, I was very pleased with how you acted today. You're really developing into a fine leader." (If his name is not Mark, don't call him that.) This will do wonders compared to ignoring appropriate behavior or saying something sarcastic like, "It's nice to see that you don't have to act like a fool all the time." It also may be appropriate to pull a student aside after class to compliment them on improved behavior since complimenting him in front of the class may embarrass him and make him revert back to bad behavior.

Appendix C

The Handshake

Although this is not a music article per se, students reading this might learn a simple lesson that could help them in big ways. This article was rejected by the Chicken Soup for the Soul people. I thought about titling this chapter "Cold Chicken Soup" but that would sound like I'm bitter. I harbor no ill feelings toward the Chicken Soup people. Everyone makes mistakes. Their books are good, but have you read some of those stories? Come on. Why they would put some of those stories in and not this one is beyond me. But life goes on. The rejection is not something I dwell on. I submitted this three years ago so I have about forgotten all the pain that their stupidity thrust upon me.

When I was in third grade, my family moved to Montgomery, Alabama. Across the street from our new home lived Mrs. Caulkins, a small, proud widow whose stern demeanor could not hide an obvious kindness that came through despite her best efforts to conceal it.

Many spring and summer days we would see her outside tending to her carefully manicured lawn, the nicest I had ever seen. Mockingbirds would serenade her as she worked, swooping down to snack on crab apples that dared land on her finely cut grass after dropping from one of six trees lining the front of her yard. I often dreamed of being able to play football on that immaculate surface. I would have felt like a professional playing on artificial grass!

Her yard was simply an extension of her overall meticulousness. The trimmed shrubbery, the pristine condition of the furniture in her house, and the ever-sparkling pink Cadillac in her carport all testified to her sense of organization and detail.

Small talk while doing yard work gradually led to a friendship between her and our family that was rather unusual, the 60's being a time when many were withdrawing into the sanctity of their own homes, the word "neighbor" just starting to lose its meaning. Her children lived some distance away, and, despite her independent spirit, I know she valued our friendship.

After I completed elementary school, our family moved to Auburn, Alabama. We returned to Montgomery two years later. Now living in a different part of town, we decided to visit Mrs. Caulkins.

As we pulled into her driveway, we could see the still perfectly manicured lawn and plants. Her shiny pink Cadillac was still in the carport, its odometer not

Appendix C

far advanced from when we left two years earlier. The mockingbirds were long gone, their prime hangouts having disappeared years before when Mrs. Caulkins, tired of cleaning up fallen crabapples, had them removed.

She greeted us graciously, yet formally, a hug being out of the question. She extended her hand to each one of my family and as she took my hand, her face soured considerably. Looking up at me (for I had grown considerably over the last two years) she said, "Don't put your hand out like it's an old, dead fish. A man should always give a firm handshake." A firm satisfaction showed on her face as I tried again.

Wham. Right between the eyes. No long lecture on how important a handshake can be—just two short sentences that I would never forget. For years I shook hands firmly for no other reason than the fact that Mrs. Caulkins told me not to put my hand out like an "old, dead fish."

I now realize the importance of the handshake. A solid handshake shows confidence. Mike Ditka, former coach of the New Orleans Saints, lost all interest in a prospective college running back after shaking hands with him. "Like shaking hands with a dead fish," Ditka commented.

A handshake can convey trust; many agreements are sealed with the familiar "Let's shake on it." A handshake can symbolize the reconciliation of conflicts and the desire to maintain peace. It can also show respect.

A warm handshake tells others we care about them. It can convey love. Louis Armstrong explains it best when he sings in "What a Wonderful World":

"I see friends shaking hands, saying, 'How do you do?' They're really saying, 'I love you.'"

I doubt there has been a handshake since that day many years ago that I have not thought of Mrs. Caulkins. Many times I accept a limp offering of some young person and smile, thinking of what she would say about the "old, dead fish" they were holding out. While not as blunt as she no doubt would be, I often follow such "old, dead fish" handshakes with the story of Mrs. Caulkins. I am passing on her very short but lifelong lesson — one handshake at a time.

Appendix D

For Students Only
25 Ways to Mess with a Band Director's Mind

1. Hum the tuning note slightly below pitch while your director is tuning another player.

2. Brass players, pop the mouthpiece with a cupped hand. (Also ask your director to get stuck mouthpiece out after class.)

3. Woodwind players, say, "It's the reed, not me!" every time you make a mistake, even on missed rhythms.

4. March like one leg is shorter than the other.

5. When the band gets back from a long trip, be the last one to leave, approximately one hour after the band's return.

6. Ask to use the bandroom phone every day after school.

7. Wear a fake cast on your leg the day before a marching competition.

8. Act like your bassoon is attacking you and wrestle it to the ground.

9. Talk to your instrument. Give it a name.

10. Ask a question your director just answered.

11. Brass players, loosen up valve caps and clack valves up and down.

12. Play a "stinger" at the end of a march that doesn't have one.

13. Act like you are going to play a stinger by using a strong up and down motion.

Appendix D

14. Section leaders, assign section members a time to miss a key signature in the same spot.

15. Brass and percussion players, take turns dropping a drumstick or mute right before the downbeat of each song.

16. Jazz up your tuning notes.

17. During marching band, carry a thermometer around your neck and say, "It's hot!" every five minutes.

18. Make a really awful mistake on the final run-through (preferably a spot that has never had problems before).

19. Every time your director turns away from you, give a "Heil, Hitler!" salute and mouth, "Mein Fuhrer!"

20. Find out what your director's least favorite song is and play it over and over again. Teach it to the whole band. Good song choices: "Barney Song," "The Hokey Pokey," "This is the Song That Never Ends," and the *Jaws* theme.

21. Drummers, leave the snare strainer off every time you begin a march and say, "Oops! My bad!" each time.

22. Constantly look around the bandroom with a sly smile on your face.

23. Quiet and shy kids, go up and insult the band director and don't say anything again for another month until you insult him again.

24. Say "Are we there yet?" every five minutes of a band trip, even ones that are only fifteen minutes long.

25. In the middle of an intense rehearsal, raise your hand and ask an irrelevant question:

>   a. How old are you?
>   b. When is class over?
>   c. Did you know you look like Regis Philbin?

Note to director: If it seems like I am selling out, consider two things:

(1) Most students do these things all the time anyway.
(2) If you read this, you know what to expect.

Appendix E

For Directors Only
25 Ways a Director Can Get Back at Students

1. Start referring to the trombone as the sackbut.

2. Pick your nose with your baton.

3. Recite portions of *The Iliad* before each rehearsal.

4. Pick a bass drummer to play a trumpet solo on his drum.

5. Insist that each rehearsal begin with everyone holding hands while they sing "We Are the World."

6. Act like you cut off your finger in the paper-cutter.

7. Say "one more time" and do it five more times (every day).

8. Tell them not to play any of the half notes because a new federal law prohibits their use.

9. Start "dying laughing" for no apparent reason and after about two minutes begin rehearsal again with no explanation.

10. Use a baton that is 24 inches long.

11. Curl up and take a nap on the podium in the middle of rehearsal.

12. Don't conduct the stinger on a march to see who plays solo.

13. Conduct a stinger on a march that doesn't have one.

14. Write a new alma mater based on "Louie Louie."

15. Write a drill where the woodwinds have to march thirty yards in six steps.

16. Sing Olivia Newton-John's "I Honestly Love You" over the press box sound system right before the band performs at halftime.

17. Constantly refer to them as "boys and girls" in the most elementary sing-songy voice possible.

18. Scream, "I can't take it anymore!" and roll on the floor mumbling, "I want my mommy," over and over again.

19. Demand that all players get their horns up quickly. Then have them lower them while you talk for five more minutes. Repeat.

20. Tell them that for the next fundraiser they will be selling autographed posters of the principal.

21. Tell them stories beginning with, "When I was a kid . . . "

22. "Remind" them of their test the next day (even though that is the first they have heard of it).

23. Tell the band to begin at measure 35 and when they begin playing, stop them and disgustingly say, "I said 84!" Ignore their objections.

24. When they ask for the order of the concert, add a difficult song the group has only played once.

25. At a marching competition, pull your pants up to your chest and walk nerd-like as you lead the band onto the field.

Typeface

This book was printed using the Palatino typeface designed by Hermann Zapf in 1948. This modern type is in keeping with the spirit of the Renaissance letter forms and is named after the Italian writing master of the sixteenth-century Giambattista Palatino. Zapf was born in Nuremberg, Germany in 1918 and is a book designer and creator of text faces for books, magazines, and newspapers.

Epilogue

intangible (ĭn-tăn' jə- bəl) *adj*. Incapable of being perceived, precisely defined, or identified; incorporeal; elusive.

Our world is increasingly becoming more dependent on fact and verification. Human nature drives us to search, discover, understand, and explain everything. This drive has resulted in undeniable gains for mankind, but at what cost? I fear we may be losing our respect and value for the intangible.

In music, researchers are examining the brain and the role it plays in musical development. Other researchers examine the body's genetic makeup, searching for a music gene. And while the goals of these studies are laudable, are we in danger of reducing music to a mere intellectual exercise when it is the mysteriousness of music that holds its allure? Do we risk losing the fascination of the Ancients who must have gasped in wonder at new sounds as they were discovered?

In sports, some athletes are described as having the intangibles—qualities not measured by height,

Epilogue

weight, leaping ability, or speed in the forty-yard dash. These athletes amaze others by performing in a way deemed impossible given what they look like on paper. I view music the same way. Music cannot simply be defined as notes on a page or just some biological function.

I hope music will be able to survive the scrutiny. When watching Alfred Hitchcock's films, I root for the innocent protagonist as he desperately avoids capture. In the same way, I pull for music. May it keep running and running—just out of our reach.

Index

A

Acknowledgements, xxi
Acme Eraser and Chalk Tracker, 92
Adolphe Sax, 21
AIFS, xv, xvii, xviii, xix
Albisi, Abelardo, 21
Appendix
    A, On the Selection of Music for the Marching Band, 223
    B, Basic Discipline Tips, 229
    C, The Handshake, 232
    D, 25 Ways to Mess with a Band Director's Mind, 236
    E, 25 Ways a Director Can Get Back at Students, 240
Arban, Jean-Baptiste, 128
Assignment Induced Fatigue Syndrome, xv

B

Bach, ii, 46, 120, 122, 124, 193
BB King, 20
Beethoven, 25, 132, 143
beginning band, 1, 2, 3, 37, 71, 72, 149, 178, 183, 210, 211, 212, 216, 222
Beginning Band Night, 210
Beginning Band Solo Titles and the Self-Esteem of Beginning Band Students, 14
bladder, 161
bugs, xvi, xviii, xix
    Alabama dung wasp, xvii
    orientalis kamikaze moth, xvii
    paterno bugiopolis, xvii

Bugs, xvi

C

Call of the Wild, ii, 1
charades, 178
Christmas, 57, 91, 93, 94, 128, 215
Clapton, Eric, 20
Classic Poetry Revisited, 151
Confusion, xxvii
Contents, xi
Convention Fatigue, 192
Courtois, Antoine, 21
Copland, 46
Creative Beginning Band Classes, 217

D

Dear Santa, ii
Dedication, xv
directing, 120
Double (Reed) Trouble, ii, xxvi, 38

E

Econo Oboe Mute, 94
Elvis, Presly, 119, 154
Epilogue, 245
Every Band Has One, 6

F

Fables in 4/4 Time, 134
fatigue, xv
Flesh-Toned Duct Tape, 93
fundraising, xxvii, 65
Fundraising, 169

G

Grand Serenade, 120, 121, 126
Granddaddy's Baton, 127

H

Harrison, James, 34
Haydn baryton, xxvi
Hermann, Bernard, 2

I

Implications for Band Directors, 202
improvement
    concentration, 27, 33
    listening, 32
    performance, 27
    positive characteristics, 31
    publicity, 96
insect collection, xv
inspiration
    Grandaddy, 127
    Mom, xv, xvi
    Mrs. Caulkins, 232
instrument
    baritone, 18, 125
    bassoon, 17
    clarinet, 2, 7, 15, 29, 30, 38, 70, 76, 89, 122, 124, 126, 128, 130, 131
    flute, 2, 4, 9, 15, 22, 23, 26, 60, 76, 88, 92, 152
    french horn, 3, 79, 124
    lardophone, 21
    oboe, xxvii, 2, 16, 38, 39, 40, 41, 42, 76, 94, 121, 125, 151, 159
    percussion, 19, 24, 50, 52, 53, 80, 83, 85, 92, 100, 125, 135, 170, 186, 192, 221, 238
    piccolo, 9, 82, 88, 124
    saxophone, 2, 17, 21, 34, 35, 144
    trombone, 2, 6, 18, 19, 24, 40, 41, 71, 100, 123, 152, 194, 240
    trumpet, 3, 4, 6, 8, 9, 13, 15, 17, 18, 19, 20, 22, 24, 41, 57, 61, 63, 84, 100, 108, 109, 121, 123, 126, 128, 136, 165, 177, 240
    tuba, 3, 18, 41, 88, 89, 91, 180
intangible, 245
inventors, 22, 23, 24, 26
It Goes Without Saying, 176

J

journal, private, 180

K

Key Signature Shock Device, 94

L

letter, xxvii
    confusion, xxvii
    disgruntled reader, xxvi
    eagle-eye, xxvi
    memories, xxviii
    praise, xxvii
    Siberia, xxvi
letter:, xxv
Likes and Suggestions, 206
Lombardiesque, Vince, 28

M

magazine
    MAD, 78

National Geographic, xvii
Reader's Digest, 147, 148
The Instrumentalist, 109
Twist, 161
marching band, xxv, 11, 31, 39, 40, 42, 128, 162, 180, 197, 226, 238
McGregor, Douglas, 199
Memories
    Grandaddy, 127
    James Harrison, 34
    letter, xxviii
    mom, xv
Mom, xvi, xvii, xviii, 81
Monday Night Football, 80
Motivation, 198
Move Over Mr. Holland, iii, v, viii, ix
Mozart, xviii, 46, 120
Muller, Louis, 21
Murphy the Band Director, 48
musical
    literacy, 147
My Favorite Things, 78

N

Name That Instrument, 20
Nerf Baton, 93

O

Open Letters to Piano Teachers, 185

P

paddlings, 166, 167
poems, 151
Politically Correct Band WORKS, 46
porch, xvi
programming, 192, 193
Psycho theme, 2
pythagorean, 58

Q

Quit-No-More, 93

R

Raessler, Dr. Kenneth R., 223
    Ready or Not—Your Final Test, 102
Real World University, 168
Reality Check, ii, 27
Rimsky-Korsakov, 46

S

Schickele, Peter, 120
Schubert, Franz, 133
skit
    Monday Night Football, 80
Smart Hat, 94
Sousa, viii, 46, 93, 142, 152, 153, 171, 193, 195
Student Conductors, 187
Student-Be-Gone Repellent, 94

T

Teike, 47
test, 147
    Wiseguy, 142
The Fine Art of Publicity, 96
The Instrumentalist, ii, xxii, xxviii, 48
The Mind of the Wiseguy, 140
The Politically Correct Band Director, 43

Theory X or Theory Y, 198
Thick Skin Cream, 93
Thurber James
   Fables for Our Time, 134
To the Rear, 164
Tuba Perhahandle, 91
Typeface, 244

U

ugly, outtakes, 252

V

Virtual Reality Band Trip, 94

W

Wagner, 25
Weismuller, Johnny, 3
wife, 137
wiseguy, 140, 141, 144, 145, 146
   World Book Encyclopedia, xvi

X

X,
   Theory, 198, 199, 200, 202, 203, 204

Y

Y,
   Theory, 199, 200, 202, 203, 204

Z

Zapf, 244

I'm not very photogenic. If you thought my photo on the back cover looked bad, look at these outtakes –

GIVE THE GIFT OF TREY REELY's BOOKS
TO YOUR FRIENDS AND COLLEAGUES

Check Your Local Bookstore, Music Dealers, or Order Here

☐ **YES,** I want _____ copies of *Mr. Holland Strikes Back: More Tales from the Podium* for $12.95 each.

☐ **YES,** I want _____ copies of *Move Over Mr. Holland: Insights, Humor, and Philosophy on Music and Life* for $9.95 each.

My check or money order for $_____ is enclosed.

Payment must accompany order. Allow 3 weeks for delivery.

Name: _____

Organization: _____

Address: _____

City/State/Zip: _____

Phone: (___)_____ E-mail: _____

Mail your check (payable to Trey Reely) to

Trey Reely
1200 Spring Grove Road
Paragould, Arkansas 72450

Contact the Author

Trey Reely
1200 Spring Grove Road
Paragould, Arkansas 72450

rhtreely@hotmail.com
http://www.sculptnet.com/reely/